THE INTERNATIONAL STATUS OF THE SUEZ CANAL

THE INTERNATIONAL STATUS
OF THE SUEZ CANAL

by

JOSEPH A. OBIETA, S. J.
S. J. D. (Harvard)

Professor of International Law
University of Deusto (Bilbao)

WITH A FOREWORD BY

RICHARD R. BAXTER

Professor of International Law
Harvard Law School

THE HAGUE
MARTINUS NIJHOFF
1960

PRINTED IN THE NETHERLANDS

FOREWORD

At the turn of the century, a definitive history of the Suez Canal by Charles-Roux, *L'Isthme et le Canal de Suez*, listed in its bibliography 1499 items on this major interoceanic waterway. A conservative estimate would probably set at double, treble, or quadruple this number the notes and studies on the Suez Canal which have been published since 1901. A word of explanation about a further work on the Canal may therefore be called for.

Throughout its history the Suez Canal has been the focus of controversy and conflict, arising out of attempts to control this crucial point on the sea passage linking Europe with the east coast of Africa, India, the Far East and Australasia. Much of this troubled history yields more readily to political than to legal analysis. The most important single *legal* question about the Canal concerns the dimensions of the right of free passage. That question has become of grave concern to the entire world community only with the war between the Arab States and Israel and the short-lived conflict of 1956–57 between France, Great Britain, and Israel on the one hand and Egypt on the other.

The legal literature on Suez which appeared in the period terminating with the close of the Second World War was very largely descriptive and historical, concerned with precedents for passage under various circumstances, with the peculiar juridical position of the Compagnie Universelle du Canal Maritime de Suez, and with the relationships of Egypt with other Powers. The disputed questions of the post-War period – the closure of the Canal to Israeli vessels and to ships carrying cargo to and from Israel, the effect of the Armistices of 1949, the nationalization of the Suez Canal Company, and the ensuing conflict between Egypt and other States – have not for the most part been analyzed with that balance and detachment which the just and consistent solution of legal problems demands. Many of the scholarly writings may justifiably be characterized as special pleadings for one party or another. When the problems of

Suez have been discussed in legal terms, as contrasted with the
political utterances which exist in such abundance, the attempted
solution of the legal dispute has suffered from references to such
amorphous concepts as "internationalization" or the quality of being
an "international public utility." The existence of what an American
would refer to, in concepts borrowed from the Constitution of the
United States, as a "case or controversy" has thus been both a
stimulus and a deterrent to accurate legal thinking about the problem of Suez – a stimulus in terms of making the problem both im-
mediate and important and a deterrent in making the legal rights
and duties which make up the legal régime of the Suez Canal a
matter of the weightiest political and economic importance.

The central legal problem of the Suez Canal has been and con-
tinues to be the extent of the right of free passage through the waterway. The Convention of Constantinople of 1888 and the Egyptian
Declaration of April 24, 1957 have spoken unequivocally and un-
ambiguously only as to the free passage of vessels of the signatories
to the Convention of Constantinople under normal conditions prevailing in time of peace. There is no unanimity of opinion as to two
other matters of far graver concern to all those nations which rely
in one way or another upon the Suez Canal. The first of these is the
open question of the rights and remedies of States which are not
parties to the Convention in the event their ships should be denied
passage or the Convention modified to their detriment. The second
is the extent of the powers of the United Arab Republic to place
restrictions on passage in the interests of its national security, by
way of closing the Canal, of excluding certain vessels, or of seizing
various categories of ships and cargo found in the Canal.

In this volume, Father Obieta expresses the view that the Concession of 1856, seen in its diplomatic context, was a unilateral
declaration which, through acceptance by the international community, imposed on Egypt and its successor, the United Arab Republic, a duty to afford free passage to the merchant ships of all
nations in time of peace. A corresponding right to freedom of passage
for warships he finds only in the terms of the Convention of Constantinople and then only as to the warships of parties to the treaty,
since other nations neglected to adhere to the Convention. These
views are deserving of particular attention, representing as they do
a departure from the commonly held, and perhaps unthinkingly
accepted, view that the rights and duties of all nations find their

origin and their measure in the Convention of 1888. The author
identifies the Egyptian Declaration of 1957 as being, at least tenta-
tively and temporarily, the current source of the right of free passage.
The author considers that, as to the second question – the defensive
rights of the territorial sovereign – the practice of States, and more
particularly that of Great Britain and of Egypt as acquiesced in by
others, has given recognition to the right of the United Arab Republic to limit passage or to close the Canal in time of war, even as
against signatories to the Convention of Constantinople.

These views and other important conclusions reached by Father
Obieta are based upon a careful examination of the diplomatic
history of the Suez Canal and are judiciously related to the general
fabric of international law. The freshness of vision and the objec-
tivity which the author has brought to this study should commend
it to all who are interested in the legal status of Suez and in the
wider question of the manner in which a legal régime is established
through the conduct and agreement of States.

R. R. Baxter

The Law School of Harvard University
        Cambridge, Massachusetts
            January, 1960

TABLE OF CONTENTS

Foreword   v

List of Abbreviations   xi

Introduction   1

CHAPTER I. Historical Background   4

Section   I: The Construction of the Canal   5
Section II: The First Years of the Canal   8
Section III: The Canal under British Occupation . . .   10
Section IV: The Canal under Egyptian Control   18

CHAPTER II. International Canals   22

Section   I: Definition   22
Section II: The Establishment of the International
             Regime   26
             Problems raised when full consent is given.   27
             Problems raised when consent is given in a
             Treaty of Peace   36
             Problems raised when no consent is given .   37
Section III: Legal Nature   39
Section IV: Legal Consequences   43

CHAPTER III. The Suez Canal from 1854 to 1888: The Inter-
             national Canal   48

Section   I: The Intention of the Sovereign   49
Section II: The Regime of Internationality   57
Section III: The Other Regimes   61

CHAPTER IV. The Suez Canal from 1888 to 1956: The Neutralized Canal   66

Section   I: The New Regime   66
Section   II: Legal Effects of the Convention   70
Section III: The Convention in the Practice of States. .   78
Section IV: Legal Consequences   87

CHAPTER V. The Suez Canal since 1956: The Nationalized Canal   90

Section   I: Legal Character of the Canal Company . .   91
Section   II: Effects of Nationalization on the Legal Regime of the Canal   103
Section III: Legal Guarantees Concerning the International Regime   107

CONCLUSION : The Future   111

APPENDIX A : The Concession of 1856   114

APPENDIX B : The Constantinople Convention of 1888 . . .   119

APPENDIX C : Security Council's Resolution of October 13, 1956   123

APPENDIX D : Egyptian Declaration of April 24, 1957 . . .   124

Bibliography   128

Index   132

LIST OF ABBREVIATIONS

A.F.D.I.:	Annuaire Français de Droit International.
A.J.I.L.:	American Journal of International Law.
ANNUAIRE:	Annuaire de l'Institut de D. International.
ANNUAL DIGEST:	Annual Digest and Reports of Public International Law Cases.
B.C. PRIZE CASES:	British and Colonial Prize Cases.
B.F. St. PAP.:	British and Foreign State Papers.
DOCUMENTS:	Documents on International Affairs. Royal Institute of International Affairs.
DOC. DIPL.:	France, Ministère des Affaires Etrangères, Documents Diplomatiques.
I.C.J.:	International Court of Justice.
J.D.I.P.:	Journal du Droit International Privé (Clunet).
L.N.T.S.:	League of Nations Treaty Series.
PARL. PAP.:	Great Britain, Parliamentary Papers.
P.C.I.J.:	Permanent Court of International Justice.
RECUEIL:	Recueil des Cours. Académie de Droit International, La Haye.
R.D.I.L.C.:	Revue de Droit International et de Législation Comparée.
R.D.I.S.D.P.:	Revue de Droit International, de Sciences Diplomatiques et Politiques.
R.G.D.I.P.:	Revue Générale de Droit International Public.
SURVEY:	Survey of International Affairs. Royal Institute of International Affairs.
U.N.T.S.:	United Nations Treaty Series.
U.S. FOR. REL.:	Papers relating to the Foreign Relations of the United States.

INTRODUCTION

On November 17, 1869, amid the splendour of celebrations and in the presence of royal families and dignitaries from practically all countries of the world, the Suez Canal was officially opened to the navigation of vessels of all nations present and future.

The event marked the beginning of a new era in the field of international communications. During the next half century three more interoceanic canals were inaugurated, the Corinth Canal in 1893, the Kiel Canal in 1895 and the Panama Canal in 1914.

The impetus thus given to the construction of interoceanic canals had also its counterpart in the field of legal theory. An increasing interest in the study and regulation of international waterways was made manifest not only by the resolutions passed by the learned societies, such as the *Institut de Droit International*[1] or the *Inter-Parliamentary Union*,[2] but above all by the Conventions and international Treaties concluded by the great Powers, among which the Constantinople Convention of 1888[3] and the Barcelona Conventions of 1921[4] are the most conspicuous illustrations.

The important effects, both practical and legal, that followed the opening of the Suez Canal, were primarily the result of two factors: first, the extraordinary commercial success which the canal has almost always enjoyed during its life time; and second, the very peculiar circumstances which have surrounded its whole history.

Among the reasons that account for the success of the Suez Canal, its geographical location should be mentioned first. Lying, as it does, at the cross-roads between East and West, and between the markets of industrialized Europe and the raw materials of under-developed Asia, the Suez Canal was necessarily bound to attract the bulk of the commercial traffic of the world. In 1870, the first year after the Canal

---

[1] Sessions of September 1878. *Annuaire*, v. 3 (1), pp. 111–118 and 328–350.
[2] Conférence de La Haye, 1913. Union Inter-Parlementaire, *Résolutions de Conférences et Décisions Principales du Conseil*, II (1911–1934) 13 and 168–170.
[3] *Parl. Pap.*, Commercial No. 2 (1889), C.5623. See also Appendix B, below.
[4] L.N.T.S., 7 (1921–1922) 11.

was opened to navigation, the number of vessels passing through it was 486 with an aggregate net tonnage of about 436,000 tons.[1] By 1955, the last year before the Canal was nationalized by the Egyptian Government, those figures had risen to 14,666 ships with an aggregate net tonnage of over 115 million tons.[2]

On the other hand, during the fiscal year 1955-56, the Panama Canal, second only in importance to the Suez Canal, was traversed by 8,376 ships, considerably less than 2/3 the traffic of Suez, with an aggregate net tonnage of 42 millions and a half, or about 1/3 that of Suez.[3] This substantial difference between the traffic and tonnage going through each of the two most important interoceanic canals is adequately explained by the exceptional geographical location of the Suez Canal.

The Suez Canal has also proved a great success from a financial viewpoint. It would be very hard, if not impossible, to assess the exact value of all the assets of the Suez Canal Company. It suffices to say, however, that in 1955, revenue from the canal totaled almost $ 95,000,000 more than the original cost of the canal,[4] or to take another illustration, that the 176,602 shares bought by the British Government in 1875 and for which Disraeli had paid 4,000,000 pounds, were estimated in 1948 to be worth 24,592,310 pounds or about six times their original value.[5]

If the success of the Suez Canal in both its aspects, commercial and financial, has been so extraordinary, the circumstances that have surrounded its whole history are no less so. The Canal was built by a private company organized under a *Firman* or decree of the Viceroy of Egypt, in 1854, later supplemented by another one in 1856.[6] The company was granted a concession for 99 years to administer and exploit the Canal. At the expiration of the concession the Canal was to revert to the possession of the Egyptian Government upon the indemnification of the company for all the movable property.

The navigation in the Canal was from the outset the object of international agreements which culminated in 1888 in the Constantin-

[1] *Parl. Pap.*, Commercial No. 23 (1879), C.2399, p. 17.
[2] Compagnie Universelle du Canal Maritime de Suez, *The Suez Canal Company and the Decision taken by the Egyptian Government on 26th July 1956*, p. 39.
[3] U. S. A., *Panama Canal Company. Canal Zone Government. Annual Report*, Fiscal Year ended June 30, 1956, p. 62.
[4] Longgood, *Suez Story*, p. 138.
[5] Royal Institute of International Affairs, *The Middle East. — A Political and Economic Survey*, p. 171, n. 2.
[6] *B.F.St.Pap.*, 55 (1864–1865) 970 and 976.

ople Convention guaranteeing freedom of transit and navigation under conditions of perfect equality to all vessels of the world in time of peace and of war.

The strategic position of the Suez Canal has also played an important role in the diplomatic history of the last century, and has even given rise to serious international conflicts, among which the Israeli-Egyptian War of 1956 with its concomitant Anglo-French invasion is only the most recent instance.

Another trait of the Canal was the universal character of the Company put in charge of its administration, formed as it was by investors of many nations and dealing quite often with the Egyptian Government on a basis of apparent equality. This lent colour to the belief among the Egyptian people that the Company was a representative of foreign Powers which it was necessary to eliminate first, if Egypt was going to enjoy full sovereignty and independence.[1]

As a result, in part, of this belief the Suez Canal Company was nationalized on July 26, 1956. By a decree of the same date, the Egyptian Government set up a Governmental Agency to take over the administration and operation of the Canal, thus bringing to a premature end the Company's concession, which was not due to expire until November 17,1968.

The international repercussions stemming from this act are common knowledge to any person even superficially acquainted with political events. The legal issues, however, raised by the action of the Egyptian Government are of a more permanent nature and greatly interest the international community. Chief among them, and dealt with in this study, is the question of the international regime of the Suez Canal and of the right of all nations to navigate freely through it. By confining the inquiry to the legal aspect of the problem it is hoped both to be able to clarify some of the most knotty issues involved in it and to avoid the pitfalls of contemporary world politics.

However, before any of the issues involved are taken up for individual discussion, a glance at the history of the Suez Canal is necessary, in order to place those issues in their proper historical perspective.

---

[1] See the remarks made by President Nasser in his speech of July 26, 1956, to the people of Alexandria. U.S. Dept of State, *The Suez Canal Problem*, p. 29, (hereinafter cited as *The Suez Problem*).

HISTORICAL BACKGROUND

The history of the Suez Canal is a very long one.[1] From the time
of the Pharaohs, about 1900 B.C. till 776 A. D., when the last canal
was closed by order of the second Abbasid Caliph, Aben-Jafas-Al
Mansour, there seem to have been altogether no less than five canals.[2] After this date, a long period of rest followed in which the
question of the canal remained more or less dormant,[3] until it was
formally taken up again at the end of the eighteenth century.

With the landing of Napoleon in Egypt on July 1798, the history
of the Suez Canal entered into its modern phase. Napoleon's conquest
of Egypt not only made it possible to explore the practical possibilities of opening a Canal,[4] but it served also to call the attention of
the world to the strategic significance of Egypt.[5]

The French conquest of Egypt had also another and rather unexpected effect in Mehemet Ali's rise to power. An Albanian by birth,
he served with distinction in the Turkish army during the French
occupation of Egypt, proclaimed himself Viceroy in 1806, and in 1807

[1] Among the many books dealing with various aspects of the history of the Suez Canal
the following may be mentioned as particularly helpful: Charles–Roux, *L'Isthme et
le Canal de Suez*, 2 vols.; Hallberg, *The Suez Canal*; Wilson, *The Suez Canal.Its Past,
Present and Future*; Crabitès, *The Spoliation of Suez*;Schonfield, *The Suez Canal in
World Affairs*; Longgood, *Suez Story*. For full bibliographical references concerning
these and other books cited in this study, see the *Bibliography* at the end.

[2] Hallberg, *op. cit.*, ch. 1. The exceptionally favourable location of Egypt for mer-
chants and traders as "the Gate to the East" accounts sufficiently for the recurrence
of this phenomenon throughout history.

[3] The Venetians in the 16th century, the Frenchmen in the 17th, and Leibnitz in
the 18th, to mention only but a few, all entertained projects for the opening of a
canal in Egypt, but these projects never went beyond the preliminary stage of proposal and discussion. Hallberg, *op. cit.*, ch. 1 and 2.

[4] During his stay in Egypt, Napoleon ordered Le Père to survey the entire region
of the Isthmus and to report on the possibilities of reestablishing the canal. The
report was published in 1803, and exerted a profound influence upon later projects.
For a summary of its conclusions, see Charles–Roux, *op. cit.*, v. 1, pp. 147–150.

[5] Napoleon's aim in conquering Egypt was, above all, to strike at the root of English
power, the possession of India. According to the secret instruction given to him by
the Directory he was to "take possession of Egypt," "chase the English from all their
possessions in the East," and "have the Isthmus of Suez cut through." The mastery
of Egypt as a further step to world dominion was Napoleon's ultimate plan, and
remained throughout his life one of his favored ideas. Hallberg, *op. cit.*, ch. 4.

freed his new country by defeating the English. From that time until his death in 1849, he ruled Egypt as the only sovereign of the country, and deserved to be called the "founder of modern Egypt." A Firman of June 1841 granted him the hereditary viceroyalty of Egypt under the suzerainty of Turkey, which was later confirmed by the London Protocol of July of the same year.[1]

Mehemet Ali, torn between the desire to have the canal built as a source of revenue for Egypt and the fear of provoking foreign intervention, or perhaps even the occupation of Egypt by some Power, if the canal were ever constructed, never consented to the granting of a concession for its construction.[2] His successor Abbas Pasha followed in general the policies of his predecessor.

Section I THE CONSTRUCTION OF THE CANAL

Upon the accession of Said Pasha to power in 1854, Ferdinand de Lesseps, with whom the new Viceroy had been connected in his youth, was invited to Egypt, and shortly after his arrival, on November 30, 1854, obtained a Concession for the construction of a canal through the Isthmus of Suez.[3] Less than two years later, a new and more elaborate Concession was granted on January 5, 1856, that remained the basic instrument upon which the Company's right to exploit the canal rested, until the nationalization decree of July 26, 1956.[4]

The new Concession provided for the construction of a maritime canal from Suez to Peluse, a fresh-water canal connecting the Nile and the maritime canal, and two branches of the fresh-water canal directed toward Suez and Peluse.[5] The Company was to receive, free from taxes, all lands necessary for the construction of the canal, as well as the use of certain uncultivated lands, not belonging to private owners, and it was also provided that four fifths of all workers

---

[1] For the Firman, see *Parl. Pap.*, Egypt No. 4 (1879), C.2395, p. 36. For the Protocol, see Martens, *N.R.G.*, v. 2, p. 126.

[2] See Metternich, *Mémoires*, v. 8, pp. 601–603.

[3] *B.F.St.Pap.*, 55 (1864–1865) 970. English trans. in *The Suez Problem*, p. 1.

[4] *Ibid.*, pp. 976–995. See also Appendix A, below. The Concession not only approved (art. 21) but also included, as an annex, the Statutes of the Canal Company.

[5] Art. 1. By the conventions of March 18, 1863, and Jan. 30 and Feb. 22, 1866, between the Viceroy and the Company, the fresh–water canal and the branch directed toward Suez were turned over to the Egyptian Government. For these conventions see *B.F.St. Pap.*, 55 (1864–1865) 999 and 56 (1865–1866) 274 and 277.

employed should be Egyptians.[1] The Company would also enjoy tax-free the privilege of working mines and quarries as well as of import-ing, free from duties, all necessary equipment for the construction or exploitation of the canal.[2] According to Article 14, the canal would be open at all times to all ships of commerce without distinction upon payment of tolls. The Concession was to expire at the end of ninety nine years from the opening of the canal, at which date it should revert to the Egyptian Government. Finally, the Concession laid great stress upon the necessity of obtaining the Sultan's ratification before work could be started.

This last clause proved a real stumbling-block for the next ten years. The Sublime Porte under heavy pressure from England refused to grant its sanction.[3] Making no headway in Constantinople, Paris, or London, Lesseps turned to the Viceroy of Egypt asking for his leave to proceed without the Sultan's sanction.[4] Upon the Viceroy's non-committal answer, Lesseps decided to force matters to a head; on November 1858, subscriptions for the shares were opened to the public, and on April 25, 1859, work on the canal was formally begun.[5]

The diplomatic reaction that ensued took the form of a contest of influence in Constantinople between England opposing the canal and France backing Lesseps.[6] Torn between the conflicting demands of the two Powers, the Sultan, in an identical note of April 6, 1863, to Paris and London, laid down the conditions preliminary to the granting of his authorization.[7] After protracted negotiations, the

---

[1] Arts. 10 and 2. By the same convention of Feb. 22, 1866, forced labor was abol-ished, and 60.000 hectares (about 150.000 acres) of land were given back to the Egyptian Government. The Company retained some 10.000 hectares for the construc-tion of the maritime canal.

[2] Art. 13. By a convention of April 23, 1869, the Company renounced the customs franchise. *Ibid.*, 62 (1871–1872) 535.

[3] In Jan. 1858, the Turkish Minister for Foreign Affairs assured the British Ambas-sador that the Porte "will not give its consent until Her Majesty's Government sanction that undertaking." Quoted in Hallberg, *op. cit.*, p. 152.

[4] His contention was based on the precedent established by the British themselves, who during the reign of Abbas Pasha, had built a railway from Alexandria to Cairo without obtaining authorization from the Sultan. See Lesseps, *Lettres, Journal et Documents*, v. 2, p. 411, (hereinafter cited as Lesseps, *Lettres*).

[5] *Ibid.*, v. 3, pp. 84–91.

[6] Napoleon III, who in 1856 for fear of antagonizing England had left Lesseps in the cold, now, in October 1859, at the height of his power, came out strongly in favor of the canal, considering it as a French enterprise in need of official protection. *Ibid.*, pp. 235–237.

[7] These referred to the neutrality of the canal, the abolition of forced labor, and the abandonment by the Company of the adjoining lands and the fresh-water canal. *Parl. Pap.*, Egypt No. 20 (1883), C.3734, p. 4. Another despatch of a somewhat more general character had already been addressed to the same capitals on Jan. 4, 1860. *Ibid.*, p. 5, Inclosure.

Viceroy and the Company finally reached an agreement, substantially implementing those conditions.[1] The way was now clear for the granting of the Sultan's official sanction which took place by a *Firman* of March 19, 1866.[2] From then on, work on the Canal proceeded at a rapid pace, making it possible to celebrate its truly magnificent inauguration on November 17, 1869.[3]

The newly built Canal was entrusted for its administration and exploitation to a private Company, known as the *Compagnie Universelle du Canal Maritime de Suez*, and whose first President was Ferdinand de Lesseps.[4] Legally, the Company was an Egyptian corporation, subject to the laws of Egypt, but ruled in all internal matters by the French law of corporations. Its central office was located in Alexandria, and its legal and administrative offices in Paris. The capital was fixed at 200,000,000 francs, divided into 400,000 shares, at 500 francs each.[5]

The Company was governed by three different organs. The General Assembly of Shareholders, which met annually, and in which all shareholders possessing at least twenty-five shares were entitled to vote, but no shareholder was to have more than ten votes. The Board of Directors (Conseil d'Administration), an administrative body of thirty-two members representing the nations chiefly interested in the enterprise and meeting at least once a month. Finally, there was

---

[1] The agreement, drawn up in two Conventions of Jan. 30 and Feb. 22, 1866, was based on the arbitral award handed down by Napoleon III in July 1864, to whom both the Viceroy and the Company had agreed the previous February to submit their differences. See above, p. 5, n. 5. For the arbitral award, which dealt mainly with the amount of compensation to be paid the Company for renouncing its rights under the 1856 Concession, see *B.F.St.Pap.*, 55 (1864–1865) 1004.

[2] *Ibid.*, 56 (1865–1866) 293.

[3] Lesseps, *Lettres*, v. 5, pp. 318–351.

[4] Concession of 1854, Preamble and Art. 1; Conces. of 1856, Art. 21; Statutes of the Canal Company.

[5] Lesseps's intention had been that all important nations would have an equal participation in the new Company. Unfortunately, most of the Great Powers ignored his invitation. The subscription, which took place in November, 1858, was as follows:

France	207.111 shares	Netherlands	2.615 shares
Belgium	324 shares	Portugal	5 shares
Denmark	7 shares	Prussia	15 shares
Naples	97 shares	Tunis	1.714 shares
Ottoman Empire	96.517 shares	Piedmont	1.353 shares
Barcelona	4.046 shares	Switzerland	460 shares
Rome	54 shares	Tuscany	176 shares
			314.494

In May 1860, the Viceroy who had already subscribed for 64.000 shares, accepted all the still unsold shares, bringing thus his total subscription to 177.642 shares. Lesseps, *Lettres*, v. 3, pp. 2–3 and 370–371.

the Executive Committee, made up of the President and four members of the Board, which met at least once a week, and whose function was to have direct charge of the Company's business.

In order to ensure the proper understanding between the Company and the Egyptian Government, both the Concession and the Statutes provided for a Superior Agent and Chief of Services, who residing at Alexandria, should represent the Company in all its relations with the Egyptian Government, while at the same time, a special Commissioner was to be appointed by the Egyptian Government to the admistrative office of the Company at Paris, in order to take cognizance of its operations and represent there the rights and interests of the Egyptian Government.[1]

Section II   THE FIRST YEARS OF THE CANAL

From a historical viewpoint, the narrative of the Suez Canal after its inauguration may be divided in three parts: first, the period that runs from 1869 until the British landing in Egypt in 1882; second, the period of the British occupation until the treaty of 1954; and third, the period after the evacuation of the British troops in 1954. An attempt will be made here to describe the principal forces or elements which shaped the history of the Canal in each of the three periods mentioned.

The first period witnessed the rise of British interest in the Canal and the increasing European interference in Egyptian affairs. Although England had been the strongest opponent of the Canal's project, British shipowners were quick to take advantage of the new route to India once the canal was constructed. From the very beginning, British shipping through the canal secured first place, with 71 % of the total; a figure which tended only to increase in subsequent years.[2] By 1875 British interest in the Canal had become so widespread, that there was general rejoicing in England when Disraeli got hold of almost half of the shares of the Canal Company.[3]

---

[1] Conces. of 1856, Art. 9; Statutes of the Canal Company, Arts. 42 and 76; Convention of Feb. 22, 1866, Art. 14.

[2] *Parl. Pap.*, Commercial No. 23 (1879), C.2399, p. 17.

[3] Financial difficulties forced the Khedive Ismail Pasha to sell his shares of the Canal Company amounting to 176.602 and representing 44% of the Company's capital. Disraeli paid four million pounds for them. *Ibid.*, Egypt No. 1(1876), C.1391, p. 7.

The purchase of the shares manifested outwardly the inner change that had gradually taken place in British policy with regard to the Canal. It made clear, too, that Egypt was no longer master in her own house, but helplessly subject to foreign interference both in its internal and in its external affairs.

When war broke out between Russia and Turkey in 1877, the British Government served notice to both belligerents that it would not allow any blockade or interference with the Canal or its approaches, though Turkey was at the time the only legal sovereign of Egypt.[1]

In the light of this background of foreign interference, Arabi's nationalist revolt must be explained. Aggrieved by the privileges and concessions enjoyed by Europeans and Turks alike, he decided to take the whole matter to the people.[2] Mostly through his efforts, a nationalist movement arose, and rallied under the slogan "Egypt for the Egyptians." In September 1881, following a long period of continued friction between the army and the Viceroy, Colonel Arabi with 2,500 troops surrounded the palace and demanded from Tewfik the dismissal of the ministers, the convocation of the chamber, and the increase of the army.[3]

The Powers thought that some sort of intervention was necessary, and on June 2, 1882, the French and British Governments proposed the convocation of a Conference at Constantinople to deal with the threatening situation in Egypt,[4] but before any measure could be devised, a riot broke out at Alexandria on June 11th, in which more than fifty Europeans were killed.[5] This made intervention inevitable.

Arabi, to whom the defence of the country was entrusted, started preparations to resist a foreign invasion by fortifying Alexandria. Upon his refusal to discontinue work on the fortifications, Admiral Seymour on July 11th opened fire, and demolished the forts.[6] British troops were subsequently landed to quell a riot, and a few weeks later Admiral Hoskins was given permission by the Khedive "to oc-

---

[1] *Ibid.*, Russia No. 2 (1877), C.1770, p. 1.
[2] In addition to the Europeans whose number had increased enormously in the nineteenth century and who enjoyed extra–territorial privileges, such as the use of their own courts and exemption from many taxes, there were the Turks and Circassians, who held the highest posts in the army. *Ibid.*, Egypt No. 4 and No. 6 (1882), C.3188 and C.3237.
[3] *Ibid.*, Egypt No. 3 (1882), C.3161, p. 1.
[4] *Ibid.*, Egypt No. 11 (1882), C.3295, p. 6.
[5] *Ibid.*, p. 43.
[6] *Ibid.*, Egypt No. 17 (1882), C.3391, p. 120.

cupy such points of the Isthmus of Suez as you may deem useful for the free traffic on the Canal."[1] The final act took place on September 13th, when General Wosley defeated Arabi at Tel-el-Kebir. A few days later, British troops entered Cairo, and Egypt became *de facto* a British protectorate, although legally she still was under the suzerainty of Turkey.[2]

Section III   THE CANAL UNDER BRITISH OCCUPATION

The "security of the canal" had furnished the pretext for the landing of British troops on the Isthmus in August 1882, and the protection to be accorded to the Canal made it "imperative" for England to remain in Egypt. Once occupying of the country, the British began to organize their new *de facto* protectorate.

The new situation had a profound impact in two opposite directions. In England, it gave rise to a feeling of self-assurance and exhilaration. Under its influence a popular agitation began for the construction of a second canal, now that they were in occupation of the country.[3] British shipowners resented the fact that British commerce, though easily first in the use of the canal, was actually controlled by a French Company, and the country at large could not forget the spirited resistance and the threats uttered by Ferdinand de Lesseps when the British troops had landed on the Isthmus.

Eventually, the whole agitation subsided, but it served to exacerbate the feelings of resentment that the occupation of Egypt had produced in the diplomatic world. France, of her own accord, had not taken part in the bombardment of Alexandria. When, however, the British occupied Egypt and started to organize the country, France began to entertain some misgivings about England's intentions with regard to Egypt. A permanent occupation of the country would upset the traditional balance of power in the Orient; and in addition, the freedom of navigation in the canal might be jeopardized.

To allay, at least in part, these fears, Lord Granville, the British Foreign Minister, addressed a circular dispatch to the Powers in January 1883, proposing a Convention that would ensure freedom of passage through the canal to all ships in any circumstances.[4] Noth-

---

[1] *Ibid.*, p. 311, Inclosure in No. 618.
[2] *Ibid.*, Egypt No. 18 (1882), C.3401, Nos. 130 and 146.
[3] *Ibid.*, Egypt No. 17 (1883), C.3698, *passim.*
[4] *Ibid.*, Egypt No. 2 (1883), C.3462, p. 34.

ing came out of this proposal, but two years later, at the suggestion
of the French Foreign Minister, the Representatives of the Powers
in London signed a *Declaration* on March 17, in which it was decided
that a committee of Experts should assemble in Paris to draft a
definitive agreement regulating the status of the canal.[1] By this time,
France had become wholly alarmed by England's procrastinating
tactics with regard to evacuation, and was, therefore, anxious to
remove the principal reason for the British occupation of Egypt by
placing the security of the canal in the hands of an international
organ. With this purpose in view, the French project provided for
an international commission, composed of representatives of the Powers, which would be responsible for the protection of the canal and
for the execution of the treaty.[2] The provision proved wholly unac-
ceptable to the British delegates; finally, when a draft agreement
was signed in June 1885, a British reservation rendered it practically useless.[3]

For the next two years, France kept pressing England to resume
negotiations in order to reach a definitive conclusion. At last, by a
note of August 19, 1887, the British Government showed themselves
ready to accept some of the proposals put forward by the French
Foreign Minister.[4] This paved the way to the final Convention, that
was formally signed at Constantinople on October 29, 1888, by the
representatives of Great Britain, Germany, Austria-Hungary, Spain,
France, Italy, The Netherlands, Russia and Turkey.[5]

On entering upon the negotiations that led finally to this Convention, the British Government renewed the reservation made at the
Paris Conference of 1885. This meant, in effect, that the Convention
would remain in abeyance so long as England did not choose to leave
Egypt.[6] And as time went by, and there was no sign of any early

---

[1] *Ibid.*, Egypt No. 6 (1885), C.4339, Inclosure in No. 1.
[2] *Ibid.*, Egypt No. 19 (1885), C.4599, p. 72.
[3] For the text of the agreement, see *Ibid.*, p. 309. The British reservation read as
follows: "Sir Julian Pauncefote...désire, en même temps, rappeler à l'attention de
ses collègues le fait...que la Sous–Commission s'est interdit d'examiner dans quelle
mesure le Traité qu'elle préparait était compatible avec l'état transitoire et excep-
tionnel où se trouve actuellement l'Egypte. Aussi les Délégués de la Grande–Bretagne
...pensent–ils qu'il est de leur devoir de formuler une réserve générale quant à
l'application de ses dispositions, en tant qu'elles ne seraient pas compatibles avec
cette situation, et qu'elles pourraient entraver la liberté d'action de leur Gouvernement
pendant la période de l'occupation de l'Egypte par les forces de Sa Majesté Britan-
nique." *Ibid.*, p. 292.
[4] *Ibid.*, Egypt No. 1 (1888), C.5255, p. 28.
[5] *Ibid.*, Commercial No. 2 (1889), C.5623. See also Appendix B, below.
[6] See below, ch. 4, sect. 2.

evacuation by the British troops, France felt cheated, and became incensed. She had been squeezed out of Egypt, and outmaneuvered again and again by England, which now held virtually exclusive control over the Canal, the very embodiment of French ingenuity. France was not alone in her resentment, for most of the Powers shared, to a greater or lesser extent, in her feelings of bitterness and opposition to Great Britain, which led gradually, in the coming years, to the isolation of this country. On the other hand, the situation was far from satisfactory to England. As a student of this question has aptly said, describing the diplomatic outlook at the end of the century, "Egypt was like a noose around the British neck, which any Great Power could tighten when it wanted to squeeze a diplomatic concession from the Mistress of the Seas..."[1]

The root of the difficulty lay in the fact that the Canal had become indispensable to the British Empire, and that, consequently, nothing short of actual British control would assuage the anxiety felt for its security. So long as France failed to understand this vital need, there were bound to be friction between the two countries, and constant recrimination against British unwillingness to withdraw. As soon, however, as France dropped her claim for withdrawal, and accepted with resignation, if not with alacrity, the fact of the British occupation of Egypt, agreement was promptly reached. This took place in the now famous Anglo-French Agreement of April 8, 1904, that changed the whole picture of European diplomacy overnight.[2]

In return for a free hand in Morocco, France agreed to the following Article 1 of the *Declaration Concerning Egypt and Morocco*:

"His Britannic Majesty's Government declare that they have no intention of altering the political status of Egypt. The Government of the French Republic, for their part, declare that they will not obstruct the action of Great Britain in that country by asking that a limit of time be fixed for the British occupation or in any other manner..."

On her side, England, by Article 6, consented to withdraw her reservation to the Convention of 1888. Similar declarations, containing the substance of Articles 1 and 6, were signed in the following months by Germany, Italy and Austria-Hungary.[3] This way the anomalous position of Great Britain in Egypt, that had for many years poisoned her diplomatic relations with the other powers, was at last given a

---

[1] Fay, *The Origins of the World War*, v. 1, p. 126.
[2] *Parl. Pap.*, France No. 1 (1904), Cd. 1952, Inclosure 1.
[3] *Ibid.*, Egypt No. 1 (1905), Cd. 2409, p. 4.

certain legal basis as an internationally recognized *de facto* situation. England's status in Egypt became virtually a Protectorate in all but in name.

That England considered herself the sole ruler of Egypt had been clearly shown, even before the Anglo-French Agreement of 1904, in the establishment of the Anglo-Egyptian Condominium over the Sudan in 1899 without any reference to the sovereign rights of the Turkish Empire[1]; the same was also demonstrated by the Sinai incident of 1906, in which the Sultan was prevented, by sheer show of force, from stationing troops on the Sinai Peninsula and constructing a railway on his own territory, on the grounds that they would prove a menace to the liberties of Egypt and to the security of the Canal.[2]

In fact, however her international status might have been qualified in legal theory, Egypt had for all purposes become part and parcel of the British Empire. On August 5, 1914, at the commencement of hostilities, a decree was issued adopting defensive measures that actually made Egypt a belligerent on the side of Great Britain.[3] On November 2nd, Sir John Maxwell, the British Commanding General, declared Egypt to be under martial law, and on the 5th, England's declaration of war against Turkey rendered the Khedive's position in relation to the Sultan impossible.[4] Consequently, on December 18th, the British Secretary of State unilaterally proclaimed Egypt a British Protectorate, and Turkish suzerainty over her to be terminated.[5] On the following day, the Khedive Abbas Hilmi, who had adhered to Turkey, was deposed, and Prince Hussein Kamel Pasha elected with the title of Sultan of Egypt.[6]

The situation created by the unilateral act of the British Government was given a legal basis four years later in the Treaties of Peace of 1919, though the Treaty with Turkey was not actually completed until 1923.[7] In the meantime, however, Egyptian nationalism, which had been increasing in intensity while the war lasted, manifested itself openly as soon as hostilities ceased.

On November 13, 1918, two days only after the Armistice with

---

[1] *B.F.St. Pap.*, 91 (1898–1899) 19.
[2] *Parl. Pap.*, Egypt No. 2 (1906), Cd. 3006, p. 11.
[3] *B.F.St. Pap.*, 109 (1915) 429.
[4] *Ibid.*, 108 (1914²) 163.
[5] *Ibid.*, p. 185.
[6] *Ibid.*, p. 186; see also 109 (1915) 437.
[7] Treaty of Versailles, Art. 147; Treaty of Saint–Germain, Art. 102; Treaty of Neuilly, Art. 63; Treaty of Trianon, Art. 86; Treaty of Lausanne, Arts. 16, 17 and 19. *B.F.St. Pap.*, 112 (1919) 1, 317 and 781; 113 (1920) 486; 117 (1923) 543.

Germany had been signed, Zaghlul Pasha the head of the Wafd party and some of his associates who claimed to represent the Egyptian people, demanded from the British High Commissioner to be allowed to proceed to London in order to lay before the Government their demands for the complete autonomy of Egypt; but their petition was not granted by the British Government in London. When, however, in March of the following year Zaghlul declared his intention of leading a delegation to lay the Egyptian aspirations before the Peace Conference of Paris, the British reply was prompt and energetic: Zaghlul with three of his associates was arrested and speedily deported to Malta. There immediately followed violent outbreaks in Egypt, involving looting, arson, murder of British officers; and finally open revolt in four provinces that came as an unexpected shock to the ill-informed Ministers of the British Government. To cope with the agitation, Zaghlul and his associates were promptly released, and a special Mission headed by Lord Milner was sent to Egypt to report on the existing situation.

As a result of the Report published by the Commission[1] and of the conversations held with the High Commissioner and several leading Egyptians including Zaghlul and some of his adherents, the British Government became finally convinced that the time had arrived for a settlement. Consequently, on February 28, 1922, a declaration was communicated to the Sultan of Egypt containing the following principles:

1. The British Protectorate over Egypt is terminated, and Egypt is declared to be an independent sovereign State.
. . . .
3. The following matters are absolutely reserved to the discretion of His Majesty's Government until such time as it may be possible by free discussion and friendly accommodation on both sides to conclude agreements in regard thereto between His Majesty's Government and the Government of Egypt:
    (a) The security of the communications of the British Empire in Egypt;
    (b) The defense of Egypt against all foreign aggression or interference, direct or indirect;
    (c) The protection of foreign interests in Egypt and the protection of minorities;
    (d) The Soudan.
Pending the conclusion of such agreements, the *status quo* in all these matters shall remain intact.[2]

Two weeks later, the British Government communicated to the

[1] *Egypt No. 1* (1921), Cmd. 1131.
[2] *Egypt No. 1* (1922), Cmd. 1592.

Powers the substance of the Declaration by a Circular Despatch, in which it was stated that "the termination of the British Protectorate over Egypt involves...no change in the *status quo* as regards the position of other Powers in Egypt itself" and that the relations between the British Empire and Egypt were considered so vitally important to the former that His Majesty's Government "will not admit them to be questioned or discussed by any other Power," and therefore, "they will regard as an unfriendly act any attempt at interference in the affairs of Egypt by another Power, and they will consider any aggression against the Territory of Egypt as an act to be repelled with all the means at their command."[1]

The Declaration of independence provided for the conclusion of agreements by friendly accommodation on the four reserved matters. When Zaghlul and the Egyptian delegation went to London in April 1924 to discuss the question with the British Government, they insisted on several basic demands, among which the renunciation by Great Britain of her claim to protect the Suez Canal held a prominent place. To this Mr. MacDonald, the Prime Minister, replied by stating in unequivocal terms the traditional British viewpoint that was to remain unchanged until the Anglo-Egyptian Agreement of 1954:

It is no less true today than in 1922 that the security of the communications of the British Empire in Egypt remains a vital British interest and that absolute certainty that the Suez Canal will remain open in peace as well as in war for the free passage of British ships is the foundation on which the entire defensive strategy of the British Empire rests... No British Government...can divest itself wholly, even in favour of an ally, of its interest in guarding such a vital link in British communications.[2]

The uncompromising attitude taken by Zaghlul Pasha brought the negotiations to an end. It was not until 1935 that a sufficiently powerful stimulus to overcome all standing differences was found in the Italo-Abyssinian war, which thus paved the way to the Anglo-Egyptian Treaty of August 26, 1936.

By the terms of this treaty Great Britain agreed to terminate the military occupation of Egypt, to exchange Ambassadors between London and Cairo, and to support Egypt's application for membership in the League of Nations, while Egypt on her side accepted an alliance with Great Britain, and authorized her to station troops in the vicinity of the Canal.[3]

---

[1] *B.F.St. Pap.*, 116 (1922) 84.
[2] *Ibid.*, 119 (1924) 188.
[3] *Ibid.*, 140 (1936) 179.

The Treaty was to run for twenty years; however, with the consent of both parties negotiations for its revision might be entered into after ten years. In contrast to the unilateral Declaration of 1922, the Treaty of 1936 represented for the Egyptian people the official acceptance of Egypt as a sovereign and independent state by the international community.

As a result of it, relations between Great Britain and Egypt were for a time friendlier than they had been for many years past. In September 1939, however, the second World War broke out, and with it the military alliance between Great Britain and Egypt, which formed an essential part of the 1936 Treaty, came into practical operation. Egypt, though officially neutral until February 1945,[1] was practically dragged into the war from the outbreak of hostilities, and was made to endure all the unpleasant consequences derived from a state of war. Her territory was invaded and partly occupied by the German troops, the Suez Canal was repeatedly bombed and mined by German airplanes, and the whole country took the appearance of a military camp where ultimate control lay with the Allied authorities, rather than of a sovereign independent state.

On the other hand, the initial triumph of the Axis, which opened up the prospect of a final German victory, and the nationalist desire to play an independent role even at the time of the war, made the Egyptian Government hesitate to commit themselves irrevocably to Great Britain; and this, in turn, led the British authorities to interfere freely in Egypt's internal affairs.[2]

This unfortunate experience with the working of the Anglo-Egyptian alliance during the war could not but deepen Egyptian resentment of military occupation and foster the nationalist aim of getting rid once and for all of the last vestiges of British tutelage. These popular aspirations found official expression and endorsement after the war in an Egyptian note delivered on December 20, 1945, the operative part of which reads as follows:

"...now that the circumstances which determined the particular character of the treaty of 1936 have changed, it has become necessary to revise it in order to bring it into harmony with the new international situation; its clauses which

---

[1] Egypt, Ministère de la Justice, *Recueil des Lois, Décrets et Rescrits Royaux* (1945), p. 23.

[2] In June 1940 and again in 1942 the British Ambassador in Cairo forced King Farouk to entrust the Government to a person friendly to Great Britain. See *Survey 1939–1946*, The Middle East in the War, pp. 209–210 and 259.

detract from the independence and the dignity of Egypt no longer correspond to present conditions..."[1]

In consequence they asked the British Government to fix a date for the opening of negotiations.

Amid an atmosphere of mistrust and violence, negotiations opened in Cairo and continued later in London for almost a year without reaching a settlement. Failure to agree on the future status of the Sudan was, ostensibly, the reason for the break-down; but the disagreement lay much deeper. For Egypt it was a question of national prestige to terminate as soon as possible all British occupation, whereas for Great Britain the preservation of her pre-eminent position in the area was essential for the security of the Middle East.[2]

Under these circumstances, the Egyptian Government decided on July 8, 1947, to bring the matter before the Security Council.[3] In the discussion that followed, the basic Egyptian contention that the 1936 Treaty had "outlived its purpose,"[4] and was, therefore, no longer valid, was supported by Syria, Poland and the Soviet Union, but rejected by the other states. A Brazilian resolution calling for a resumption of "direct negotiations" between the parties concerned failed to obtain the seven votes required. A Colombian resolution on somewhat broader lines met a similar fate. Since there was no other proposal on the table, the Council on September 10 decided to adjourn, leaving the Egyptian question still unsolved.[5]

The failure of the Security Council to redress Egyptian grievances, followed within a year by the humiliating defeat suffered at the hands of a numerically inferior Israeli army and by the shocking disclosures of widespread corruption and cowardice in high governmental circles, threw the country into a state of bewilderment, which greatly strengthened nationalist fanaticism among the different elements of the population.

One result of this state of affairs was an increase in anti-foreign sentiment, which reached its climax in the burnings and killings of "Black Saturday" on January 26, 1952.[6] Another result was the revolution of July of the same year, by which King Farouk was forced

---

[1] *The Times* of London, Jan. 31, 1946, p. 3.
[2] 481 *H. C. Deb.* (5th ser.) 36 (1950–1951).
[3] U.N. Sec. Council, *Off. Rec.*, 2nd year, No. 59, p. 1343.
[4] *Ibid.*, No. 70, p. 1753.
[5] *Ibid.*, No. 88, p. 2363.
[6] See *Survey 1951*, pp. 282–292.

to abdicate, and which was followed within a year by the proclamation of the Republic of Egypt.

The new Egyptian Government quickly entered into negotiations with Great Britain, which paved the way to the definitive Anglo-Egyptian Agreement of October 19, 1954.[1] According to its provisions, Great Britain agreed to withdraw all British troops from Egyptian territory within a period of twenty months and declared the 1936 Treaty to be terminated, while Egypt, on her part, consented to a British return to the Suez Canal Base in the event of an armed attack on any of the Arab League States or on Turkey. The Agreement was to run for seven years, and might not be extended except by consent of both parties.

Section IV   THE CANAL UNDER EGYPTIAN CONTROL

The revolution of 1952 and the success which accompanied its first years in power altered profoundly the circumstances of the country. Once the political liberation of Egypt had been achieved by the Treaty of 1954, it was only natural that the revolutionary leaders would look forward to achieving also the economic liberation of the country; and this meant in the concrete the nationalization of the Suez Canal.[2]

The occasion was provided by the sudden refusal of the U.S. Department of State on July 19, 1956, to finance the Aswan Dam on the Nile,[3] after it had agreed to do so, followed the next day by a similar refusal on the part of Great Britain and the World Bank. Pesident Nasser retaliated within a week by a Presidential Decree of July 26, which nationalized the Suez Canal Company.[4]

The act of nationalization and the way in which it was carried out gave rise to a strong diplomatic reaction throughout the Western world. France, Great Britain and the U.S.A., after consulting with each other, decided to hold a Conference in London, to which twenty-

---

[1] *U.N.T.S.*, 210 (1955) 24.

[2] "The Suez Canal has always been regarded by Egypt and the Egyptians as their symbol of freedom from foreign domination...The awakening of the national consciousness in Egypt has made the act of the Concession to the Suez Maritime Canal Company to be viewed as an intolerable mortgage on Egyptian public life." Letter from the Representative of Syria to the President of the Security Council, *Doc. S/3674.*

[3] U.S. *Dept. of State Bulletin*, v. 35, N. 892 (July 30, 1956), p. 188.

[4] *The Suez Problem*, pp. 30–32.

one other nations were invited, to discuss the new situation and establish an international system to operate the canal.[1] Egypt, later followed by Greece, refused to attend the Conference insisting that it had "no right in any way to discuss any issue concerning the sovereignty of any of her parts."[2] At the Conference, which lasted from August 16 to 23, several delegations put forward various proposals, but a majority of 18 nations agreed in the end that the so-called Five-Power Proposal be placed before the Egyptian Government as a basis for future negotiation.[3] For this purpose, a committee of five members proceeded to Cairo at the beginning of September; President Nasser, however, rejected their proposal.[4]

On September 10, an Egyptian invitation for a new Suez Conference was sent to a number of governments.[5] The three Western powers, however, thought the Egyptian memorandum unsuitable as a basis of negotiations, and decided of their own accord to convene a second Conference in London for the purpose of establishing a Suez Canal Users Association. The Conference, which met from September 19 to 21 against strong Egyptian opposition,[6] drew up in the end a vague and inconclusive Declaration which, actually, left the whole problem where it had stood for the last two months.[7]

Under these circumstances, Great Britain and France brought the Suez question to the attention of the Security Council.[8] After protracted discussions and negotiations in public and in private, the Council by a unanimous Resolution of October 13 agreed on six principles as the basis of any settlement of the Suez question.[9] The Resolution was followed by further negotiations among the three Governments of Great Britain, France and Egypt through the good offices of the Secretary-General, and by the end of the month the points on which there still was some disagreement had been narrowed down to a few issues of rather minor import.[10] This was the situation on October 29 when Israel invaded Egypt.

The invasion was followed the next day by a twelve-hour Anglo-

---

[1] *Ibid.*, pp. 42–43.
[2] *Ibid.*, p. 52.
[3] *Ibid.*, pp. 291–293.
[4] *Ibid.*, pp. 317–322. See also the Committee's Report, p. 323.
[5] *Ibid.*, pp. 327–330.
[6] Letter of 17 Sept. 1956 from the Representative of Egypt to the President of the Security Council, *Doc. S/3650.*
[7] *The Suez Problem*, pp. 365–366.
[8] U.N. Sec. Council, *Doc. S/3654.*
[9] Ibid., *Doc. S/3675.* See also Appendix C, below.
[10] *Ibid.*, Doc. S/3728.

French ultimatum requesting both belligerents to stop all warlike operations at once; when Egypt refused to accept it, Anglo-French forces started military operations in order "to bring about the early cessation of hostilities and to safeguard the free passage of the Canal."[1] In retaliation, the Egyptian Government sank more than twenty ships and tugs in the Canal, thus obstructing its free passage for an indefinite time. The Security Council, unable to adopt a Resolution, decided to call an emergency special session of the General Assembly,[2] which promptly passed several Resolutions condemning the Israeli and Anglo-French actions by overwhelming majorities.[3] On November 6, the British and French Governments announced their acceptance of the Assembly's Resolutions for a cease-fire and agreed to withdraw their troops on condition that their place would be taken up by a U.N. emergency force.[4] On December 22, British and French forces withdrew from Port-Said,[5] and on March 7, 1957, the last contingents of Israeli troops left the Sinai Peninsula.[6] The next day, the General Assembly adjourned its eleventh regular session.[7]

When the Canal was reopened at the end of April, the Egyptian Government, in order to assuage the fears expressed by some countries, published on April 24 a Declaration, to be considered as an "international instrument," purportedly embodying the six principles adopted by the Security Council.[8] On July 18, the Declaration was supplemented by the acceptance of the compulsory jurisdiction of the International Court of Justice.[9] And, lastly, on July 13, 1958, a final agreement was signed at Geneva providing for the pecuniary compensation to the shareholders of the former Suez Canal Company.[10]

While all these steps go a long way toward proving the sincerity of the public Egyptian utterances regarding the free navigation of the Canal, it is questionable whether they meet the basic needs of the international community. It may, however, be asked in this

---

[1] Anglo-French Ultimatum, 30 Oct. 1956. Watt, *Documents on the Suez Crisis*, pp. 85–86.
[2] U.N. Sec. Council, *Doc.S/3721*.
[3] U.N. Gen. Ass., (ES–I) *Resolutions* 997, 999, 1002.
[4] *Ibid., Doc. A/3306* and *Doc. A/3307*.
[5] *Ibid., Doc. A/3500*.
[6] *Ibid., Off. Rec.*, 11th sess., Plenary meetings, pp. 1314–15.
[7] On November 10, the first emergency special session of the General Assembly had decided to transfer the Egyptian question to the agenda of its eleventh regular session, which was due to open on November 12. U.N. Gen. Ass., (ES–I) *Resolution* 1003.
[8] U.N. Sec. Council, *Doc. S/3818*. See also Appendix D, below.
[9] *Ibid., Doc. S/3818/Add.1*. See also Appendix D, below.
[10] *Ibid., Doc. S/4089* (A/3898).

connection, why the Egyptian Government should take those needs into consideration at all. For, is the Egyptian Government bound to preserve freedom of navigation in the Suez Canal? If so, is the Suez Canal an international canal? But what is, after all, an international canal? To these questions the following pages will attempt to give an answer.

CHAPTER II

INTERNATIONAL CANALS

Under the name of international waterways, three related fields are usually included – international rivers, international straits and international canals. Before proceeding further, it will be convenient to define these terms in order to deal later on with their legal relationships.

Section I DEFINITION

From the viewpoint of international law the subject of international rivers received for the first time careful consideration at the Congress of Vienna of 1815. In its Final Act, the assembled plenipotentiaries approved a *Règlement pour la Libre Navigation des Rivières*,[1] Article 108 of which reads,

"Les Puissances, dont les Etats sont séparés ou traversés par une même Rivière navigable, s'engagent à régler d'un commun accord tout ce qui a rapport à la Navigation de cette Rivière..."

And by Article 109 they proclaimed that navigation in such rivers "sera entièrement libre, et ne pourra, sous le rapport du Commerce, être interdite à Personne."

Navigable rivers, therefore, which separate or traverse different States are placed by the Congress of Vienna in a special category, and in them freedom of commercial navigation must prevail. The Congress, however, did not make compulsory the application of such principles to all the rivers that fulfilled the conditions specified in Article 108.

In 1856, the Congress of Paris took a further step. By Article 15 of the Treaty of Peace of March 30, 1856, signed by the six great Powers of the time and Turkey,[2] the contracting parties not only accepted the principles of Vienna and applied them to the navigation of the

---

[1] *B.F.St. Pap.*, 2 (1814–1815) 3.
[2] Martens, *N.R.G.*, v. 15, p. 776.

Danube, but they even declared "que cette disposition fait, désormais, partie du droit public de L'Europe, et la prennent sous leur garantie."

The Treaty of Versailles of 1919, in its Article 331, enlarged the concept arrived at in Vienna by declaring international the Elbe, the Oder, the Niemen, the Danube "and all navigable parts of these river systems which naturally provide more than one State with access to the sea, with or without transhipment from one vessel to another; together with lateral canals and channels constructed either to duplicate or to improve naturally navigable sections of the specified river systems, or to connect two naturally navigable sections of the same river..."[1]

Finally, the Barcelona Conference convened in 1921 under the auspices of the League of Nations, drew up a *Convention and Statute on the Regime of Navigable Waterways of International Concern*, in which these were defined in Article 1 as,

"All parts which are naturally navigable to and from the sea of a waterway which in its course, naturally navigable to and from the sea, separates or traverses different States, and also any part of any other waterway naturally navigable to and from the sea, which connects with the sea a waterway naturally navigable which separates or traverses different States."[2]

In the long evolution which has taken place since the Congress of Vienna approved the basic charter of principles on fluvial law, the concept of international rivers, though considerably enlarged in its application, has remained basically unchanged. The existence of an international river presupposes only two conditions: first, that the river be navigable; and second, that it provide naturally more than one State with access to the sea. As the Permanent Court of International Justice has aptly said in the case of the *International Commission of the Oder*,[3] "these are the two characteristics...by which a distinction has for a long while been made between the so-called international rivers and national rivers."

International straits, on the other hand, though much in use from time immemorial, have never been subject to an international set of rules comparable to the one given by the Congress of Vienna for international rivers. It is not surprising, therefore, to find a great variety of opinion on the nature of an international strait. For some writers, like Dupuis,[4] the essential element seems to be the usefulness

---

[1] *Ibid.*, 3me Ser., v. 11, p. 323.
[2] *L.N.T.S.*, 7 (1921–1922) 35.
[3] P.C.I.J., *Ser. A*, No. 23 (1929), p. 25.
[4] Dupuis, *Liberté des voies de communication*, (*Recueil 1924*, v. I, p. 183).

of a strait to general navigation; whereas for others, like Brüel, "the volume of traffic going on between the two areas of water" would seem to be more important.[1] There are still others, among whom the late Judge Azevedo was a conspicuous exponent, who take into consideration both factors.[2]

The International Court of Justice had an opportunity to deal with the subject of international straits in the *Corfu Channel* case. In this case, the Court, after rejecting as inadequate the former theories, held that the decisive criterion for determining the nature of an international strait "is rather its geographical situation as connecting two parts of the high seas and the fact of its being used for international navigation."[3] An objective test is thus being replaced in the concept of international straits for the more or less subjective ones which prevailed before.

The Conference on the Law of the Sea which convened at Geneva in 1958 accepted in full the notion expounded by the International Court. Article 16, paragraph 4 of the *Convention on The Territorial Sea and The Contiguous Zone*, signed on April 29, 1958, states that,

"There shall be no suspension of the innocent passage of foreign ships through straits which are used for international navigation between one part of the high seas and another part of the high seas or the territorial sea of a foreign State."[4]

The two conditions required by the Court for an international strait are plainly visible in this Article. It may thus be said that the concept of an international strait, as based upon a geographical criterion, forms part now of the body of rules which constitute international law.

Unlike international rivers and straits, which are natural waterways, international canals are artificially constructed. This essentially differentiating factor has been overlooked by a number of writers, who misled by the similarity of regimes to which both international canals as well as rivers and straits are subject, have tried to find, by analogy to the latter, a geographical or physical criterion which would serve to define an international canal.

This criterion has variously been sought in the importance of the

---

[1] Brüel, *International Straits*, v. 1, p. 23.
[2] Diss. Op. in the *Corfu Channel* Case, I.C.J., *Reports 1949*, pp. 106, 107.
[3] *Ibid.*, p. 28.
[4] U.S., *Dept. of State Bulletin*, v. 38, N. 992, p. 1111.

canal to world commerce,[1] in the universal character of the capitals spent in its construction,[2] or even in its strategic or geographical location.[3] All such endeavors, however, have proved of no avail. The fact remains that the canal, being an artificially constructed waterway through the territory of a sovereign State, requires essentially the consent of such State whatever its geographical qualifications may be.

It remained for the Permanent Court of International Justice to pave the way to the right understanding of the nature of International Canals. The Versailles Treaty of 1919, already mentioned, had decided in its Article 380 that,

"The Kiel Canal and its approaches shall be maintained free and open to the vessels of commerce and of war of all nations at peace with Germany on terms of entire equality."

The meaning of this Article came up for consideration in the *Wimbledon Case*, in which the Court held that, as a result of the terms of Article 380,

"...the canal has ceased to be an internal and national navigable waterway, the use of which by the vessels of states other than the riparian state, is left entirely to the discretion of that state, and that it has become an international waterway intended to provide under treaty guarantee easier access to the Baltic for the benefit of all nations of the world."[4]

It follows that in the Court's opinion the distinction between a national and an international canal is to be found not in any geographical factor inherent to the canal but in the regime of navigation prevailing in it. If navigation is left entirely to the discretion of the territorial state, the canal is national. If, on the other hand, there is freedom of navigation internationally guaranteed for all the nations of the world, the canal is international.

The criterion thus established is not a geographical standard, but a legal one. It presupposes the existence of an international regime guaranteeing freedom of navigation for all the nations of the world. As the Permanent Court said in the same case, "the intention of the authors of the Treaty of Versailles [was] to facilitate access to the Baltic by establishing an international régime, and consequently to keep the canal open at all times to foreign vessels of every kind..."[5]

---

[1] Rossignol, *Le Canal de Suez*, p. 174; Cavaglieri, *Règles Générales du Droit de la Paix* (*Recueil 1929*, v. I, p. 434).

[2] Cammand, *Etude sur le Régime Juridique du Canal de Suez*, p. 39.

[3] Root, *Addresses on International Subjects*, p. 181.

[4] P.C.I.J., *Ser. A*, No. 1 (1923), p. 22.

[5] *Ibid.*, p. 23.

The same notion of international canals was accepted almost thirty years later by the German Supreme Court (British Zone) in the *Kiel Canal Collision Case*,[1] when it asserted that "the true characteristic of an international waterway is freedom of navigation." There is no mention in this case of any geographical criterion.

· As a result of the foregoing authoritative pronouncements, an international canal may be defined as an artificial waterway, connecting two parts of the open seas, and subject to an international regime, whereby freedom of navigation is guaranteed for the vessels of all the nations of the world. It remains now to determine the different ways in which such an international regime may be established.

Section II   THE ESTABLISHMENT OF THE INTERNATIONAL REGIME

By its very nature a canal is always an artificially constructed waterway. Before the canal was built, the piece of land over which it runs, formed part of the territory of some State. On the other hand, territorial sovereignty is an accepted and overriding principle of international law, according to which nothing may be done within the boundaries of a certain State, except with the consent of its sovereign. It follows that if a canal is to be built, the consent of the Sovereign is required; and even more so, if the canal, once constructed, is to be governed by an international regime. Unless this double consent has been given, there will be either no canal at all, if no consent was ever granted, or a purely national canal, if the sovereign consented to have the canal built but not to have it subjected to an international regime; in neither case, however, will there ever be an international canal.

The history of the Kiel Canal may serve as an illustration. In the already mentioned *Wimbledon Case*, the Permanent Court said that the Kiel Canal "having been constructed by Germany in German territory, was until 1919 an internal waterway of the state holding both banks,"[2] but that as a result of Article 380 of the Treaty of Versailles, ratified by Germany, "the canal has ceased to be an internal and national navigable waterway...and...has become an interna-

---

[1] Lauterpacht, *International Law Reports* 1950, p. 134, (hereinafter cited as Lauterpacht, *Reports*).
[2] P.C.I.J., *Ser. A*, No. 1 (1923), p. 23.

tional waterway..."[1] It is thus clear that the consent of the sovereign is absolutely essential in order to have an international canal.[2]

(a) *Problems raised when full consent is given*

Consent to an international transaction may be either express or tacit. Express consent is given in the form of unilateral declarations or of multipartite treaties. Tacit consent is deduced either from positive acts or from so-called negative acts or sufferance. It is thus necessary to analyze the legal effects of each of these forms of consent on the establishment of an international regime in canals.

The doctrine of unilateral declarations has received little attention in international law until the present time. A number of writers even refuse to deal with the subject. Its existence, however, was recognized by the Permanent Court of International Justice in the case of the *Customs Regime between Germany and Austria*, where it said that

> "From the standpoint of the obligatory character of international engagements, it is well known that such engagements may be taken in the form of treaties, conventions, declarations, agreements, protocols, or exchanges of notes."[3]

In the *Eastern Greenland Case*, the same Court accepted, at least indirectly, the binding effect of a unilateral declaration, for it held that an oral reply given by the Minister of Foreign Affairs on behalf of Norway in response to a request by the diplomatic representative of Denmark was "binding upon the country to which the Minister belongs."[4] The reply might be considered as a promise, which the Court held to be internationally binding on the party making it.[5]

Among the writers of international law three opinions on the nature of unilateral declarations seem to prevail. The first expounded by Cansacchi, holds in general that unilateral declarations produce legal effects immediately upon being made, even before they reach the party for whom they are intended. Neither reception of the declaration nor its acceptance are required. These declarations include notification, recognition, protest, renunciation, promise and offer.[6]

---

[1] *Ibid.*, p. 22.
[2] See also Cammand, *op. cit.*, p. 172; Dupuis, *op. cit.*, p. 194; Benno, *La situation internationale du Canal de Suez*, p. 109.
[3] P.C.I.J., *Ser. A/B*, No. 41 (1931), p. 47.
[4] *Ibid.*, No. 53 (1933), p. 71.
[5] See Garner, *The International Binding Force of Unilateral Oral Declarations*, (*A.J.I.L.*, 27 (1933) 493–497).
[6] Cansacchi, *La Notificazione Internazionale*, pp. 198–205.

A second group, whose outstanding exponent is Verdross and to which perhaps Guggenheim should also be ascribed, maintains that unilateral declarations do not have legal effects until they reach the person or party for whom they are intended, although they do not further require their acceptance by that party. Reception, therefore, of the declaration is required, acceptance is not required.[1]

A third opinion, held by Biscottini,[2] rejects all unilateral declarations except renunciation. According to this opinion, the legal effect of renunciation is to extinguish a right, and this can take effect as soon as the declaration has been made. The rest of the so-called unilateral declarations, offer, recognition, promise, and so on, are upon analysis nothing else than offers, since all of them require acceptance in order to produce legal effects. Now, an offer derives its legal effect not from the act of declaration but from the acceptance of the offer, and therefore from something outside the declaration itself. Consequently, unilateral declarations as such do not have legal effects in international law.

It is difficult to agree in full with Biscottini's theory. If what he intends to say is that unilateral declarations do not have complete effects by themselves without acceptance, as for instance the transfer of a right or thing in the case of an offer, or the actual performance of some action in the case of a promise, no quarrel need arise. But, because unilateral declarations do not have full effects without acceptance, it cannot be inferred that they do not have effects at all. The withdrawing of a promise, for instance, by a certain State, after the declaration has been received by the party concerned but before it has been either accepted or rejected, would necessarily entail a breach of faith, and consequently, an international delinquency. The unilateral declaration, therefore, must have had some legal effects, in so far as the State making the promise was bound not to withdraw that promise, at least during a certain time.

Summing up this rather academic discussion, it may be said that, a) renunciation is a unilateral declaration accepted by all; b) all unilateral declarations have some legal effects, at least after they have been received by the party concerned; c) it is doubtful whether unilateral declarations have complete effects without acceptance.

Turning now to the question of consent given through a unilateral

[1] Verdross, *Le Droit de la Paix*, (*Recueil 1929*, v. V, p. 437); also, *Derecho Internacional Público*, p. 139; Guggenheim, *Traité de Droit international public*, v. 1, p. 147.
[2] Biscottini, *Contributo alla Teoria deglia Atti Unilaterali nel Diritto Internazionale*, ch. 4.

declaration to the establishment of an international regime in canals, or, what amounts to the same thing, to the building of an international canal, it is easy to see that the declaration itself would be in the nature of a promise to allow freedom of navigation through the canal to all nations, a promise which would necessarily imply a partial renunciation of sovereignty over the canal, in so far as it would not be open to the sovereign any more to restrict navigation through the canal.

The declaration may take the form of an oral or written statement formally announcing the intention of the sovereign to the whole world, but it need not be so. It might even be included initially in a municipal law or decree, provided the substance of the declaration is later brought to the notice of those whom it is supposed to benefit.[1]

Since some doubts have been cast by certain writers on the value of unilateral declarations unless followed by acceptance, it has been thought appropriate for the purpose of the present study, to restrict the meaning of unilateral declarations to those only that are accepted. On this point there is complete unanimity among writers, although, of course, the full concept of unilateral declarations might suffer a severe cut on the way.

Like the declaration itself, acceptance by the party concerned may also take any form whatsoever by which the internal will to accept is outwardly manifested. The mere use of the canal by the vessels of some nation would be sufficient indication of the wish of that nation to accept the international regime. It is thus clear that an international regime may be established on a canal by consent of the territorial sovereign given in a unilateral declaration and accepted by the international community.

The international regime may also be established by a multilateral treaty providing for freedom of navigation for all nations. If the treaty is concluded among all the nations of the world, either because all of them have taken part in the treaty, or because those who did not take part have later formally acceded to it, the problem of establishing the international regime would immediately be solved. As soon as the treaty was concluded between the territorial sovereign on one side, and the international community on the other, the international regime would be established, and consequently, there would be an international canal. In practice, there is no instance of a canal having been made international in such a simple way.

[1] See Cansacchi, *op. cit.*, p. 204, n. 2.

A different case occurs when the treaty has been concluded among some States only, and a number of non-signatories never accede to it, either because there was no accession clause, or because they did not choose to take advantage of it. Such has partially been the case with the treaty of Constantinople of 1888 signed by nine States only, but to which no other nation has ever acceded.[1]

The problem that arises in this connection is a grave one. On the one hand, the treaty is supposed to give a benefit – freedom of navigation through the canal – to all nations of the world; and, on the other, the non-signatory nations do not accede to the treaty, and therefore do not participate in it. The question then is this, are those non-signatory and non-acceding States going to benefit by the provisions of the treaty? If they do benefit, do they have a right to the use of the canal? If they do have a right, how did they acquire it? What is, then, the position of those states with regard to the treaty?

The problem raised by these questions is a decisive one, for so long as the territorial sovereign is not bound to the international community as such, but only to a few of its members to allow absolute freedom of navigation for all, the canal cannot be said to be international in the sense described above, for the non-signatory nations themselves would not have a "right" to the use of the canal.

The question thus posed is only an application of another and more general problem, generally known in international law as the problem of international conventions and third states. It is necessary, therefore, to turn now briefly to it.

For many years the rule *pacta tertiis nec prosunt nec nocent* was accepted without question. Beginning with the nineteenth century a few writers in international law started to make important exceptions to that rule.[2] It remained, however, for the Permanent Court of International Justice to give an authoritative interpretation to the subject. In the case of the *Free Zones of Upper Savoy and the District of Gex* the Court said[3] that "it cannot be lightly presumed that stipulations favourable to a third State have been adopted with the object of creating an actual right in its favour. There is, however,

---

[1] *Parl. Pap.*, Commercial No. 2 (1889), C.5623.
[2] Heffter, *Le droit international public de l'Europe*, para. 83; Fiore, *Nouveau droit international public*, 2nd ed., v. II, p. 389; Despagnet, *Cours de droit international public*, 4th ed., paras. 59 and 448; Oppenheim, *International Law*, 2nd ed., v. I, para. 522.
[3] P.C.I.J., *Ser. A/B*, No. 46 (1932), p. 147.

nothing to prevent the will of sovereign States from having this object and this effect." In each case, therefore, "it must be ascertained whether the States which have stipulated in favour of a third State meant to create for that State an actual right which the latter has accepted as such."

It follows from this statement, first, that stipulations in favour of third parties may validly be adopted in a treaty between two contracting States; and secondly, that the fact of their having or not having actually been adopted depends entirely on the will of the contracting parties. On the other hand, it is not very clear whether acceptance of the stipulation by the *third party* is an essential prerequisite for the transfer of the right. The last sentence in the Court's statement, "which the latter has accepted as such," could be interpreted either as an affirmation of principle or as an assertion of fact in the particular case with which the Court was dealing. In order to avoid confusion, it is proposed to consider both cases separately.

After the decision given by the Permanent Court, no one today would deny that a stipulation in favour of a third party, followed by acceptance, can validly transfer a right. The issue, however, is not the fact, but the way in which the transfer takes place and the consequences that follow from it. Two leading opinions have been advanced by writers of international law on the present question. The first, very ably expounded by Roxburgh, holds that by the acceptance the third party accedes or adheres to the original treaty. According to him,[1] "the 'accession' or 'adhesion' clause is an offer by the contracting parties to enter into legal relationship with a third state or states; an offer, which, if accepted, constitutes a new treaty. Consequently, the rights and liabilities incurred by the third state are incurred, not under the old treaty, but under an additional treaty identical in terms with the old."

It follows that the *third party*, after acceptance, has become, for all practical purposes, a party to the original treaty, enjoying its rights and being subject to its liabilities. Acceptance may take place in a formal manner by signing the treaty in accord with the accession clause, or, in case there is no such clause, by conduct implying consent, provided it is properly evidenced.[2] There is, however, one exception made by Roxburgh, and this is that acceptance by tacit consent is

[1] Roxburgh, *International Conventions and Third States*, pp. 45–46.
[2] Caution should be taken not to confuse this conduct by which an international contract or transaction is concluded, with conduct which after a long period of time gives rise to a rule of customary law. See Roxburgh, *op. cit.*, p. 72.

impossible when the treaty contains an accession clause, since in that case the original parties have determined beforehand the way they desire the acceptance to take place.[1]

Against this theory, which seems to have gone unchallenged for over forty years, Professor Jiménez de Aréchaga has very recently raised his voice.[2] He expresses the belief that "the so-called acceptance is not the expression of consent to a second agreement but is an act of appropriation of rights derived from the treaty which contains the stipulation in favor of third states. The third party beneficiary is not supposed to ratify, adhere or accede to the treaty, but merely to appropriate or renounce the rights stipulated in its favor. The acceptance is not the origin of the right: it only deprives the original contracting parties of the power to revoke a right already vested in the third party."[3]

This profound analysis of the *stipulatio in favorem tertii* would seem to accord very fittingly with actual practice. The third party beneficiary, in case it does not take advantage of the accession clause to become a full member of the treaty, does not by the mere acceptance accede to the treaty as such, which usually covers a much wider ground, but only appropriates to itself the particular right granted in the treaty by the original parties. After acceptance, the original parties are deprived of the right to revoke the grant, but, otherwise are left entirely free to act as they please: they may even change the original treaty, provided the right or rights already granted to third parties are scrupulously preserved. The third party, on the other hand, does not have a right to the implementation of the whole treaty, but only to the preservation of the right or benefit granted in the treaty, and later appropriated through acceptance. In addition, there is no need in this theory to make any distinction between treaties with an accession clause and treaties without one. In either case, acceptance of the right granted may be given either in a formal manner or also by conduct implying consent.

So much for stipulations in favour of third parties, when followed by acceptance. The question as to whether those stipulations are valid in the absence of such an acceptance remains to be considered. As already mentioned before, it is not possible to deduce any def-

---

[1] *Ibid.*, pp. 47–51.

[2] Jiménez de Aréchaga, *Treaty Stipulations and Third States*, (*A.J.I.L.* 50 (1956) 338–357). See also Decleva, *Gli Accordi Taciti Internazionali*, pp. 44–52.

[3] Jiménez de Aréchaga, *op. cit.*, p. 353.

inite doctrine from the Court's decision on the *Free Zones* case.[1] International law, however, has long recognized some cases in which rights seem to be given to third states without their prior acceptance. These include the so-called International Settlements and Custom.

International settlements have been described by Sir Arnold McNair in the following words:

> "From time to time it happens that a group of great Powers, or a large number of States both great and small, assume a power to create by a multipartite treaty some new international régime or status, which soon acquires a degree of acceptance and durability extending beyond the limits of the actual contracting parties, and giving it an objective existence."[2]

The essential characteristic of an international settlement is that the newly-created regime or status acquires an objective existence of its own in international law, which transcends the range of the signatories, and imposes itself to the international community as such, though some at least of its members have never consented to it. As Sir H. Lauterpacht has aptly expressed it, "international settlements are incipient international legislation."[3]

The World Court has on more than one occasion recognized their existence. In the *Wimbledon* case, the Permanent Court held that as a result of Article 380 of the Treaty of Versailles the Kiel Canal had become "an international waterway...for the benefit of all nations of the world,"[4] though only 28 nations had actually signed that treaty. In the case of the *International Status of South-West Africa,* the International Court declared that "the Mandate was created... as an international institution with an international object" and that "the international rules regulating the Mandate constituted an international status for the Territory"[5]; and in his separate opinion Sir Arnold McNair quoted with approval a paragraph from the Report of the Jurists on the Aaland Islands Question, where international settlements are expressly recognized.[6]

---

[1] In his recent book *The Development of International Law by the International Court*, pp. 307–308, Sir Hersch Lauterpacht contends that the Permanent Court acknowledged in the *Free Zones* case the possibility of granting rights to third parties without any acceptance being required. He does not, however, bring any conclusive proof for his assertion, but only some, so to speak, circumstantial evidence.

[2] Sep. Op. in the *Status of South-West Africa* case, I.C.J., *Reports 1950*, p. 153. See also Roxburgh, *op. cit.*, p. 81.

[3] Lauterpacht, *The Development of International Law by the International Court*, p. 309.

[4] P.C.I.J., *Ser. A.* No. 1 (1923), p. 22.

[5] I.C.J., *Reports 1950*, p. 132.

[6] Sep. Op. in the *Status of South-West Africa* case, I.C.J., *Reports 1950*, p. 154.

In no case, however, did the International Court express itself so clearly as in the case of *Reparation for Injuries Suffered in the Service of the U.N.* To the objection that the United Nations could not bring a claim against non-members of the Organization, the Court gave the following reply,

"...the Court's opinion is that fifty States representing the vast majority of the members of the international community, had the power, in conformity with international law, to bring into being an entity possessing objective international personality, and not merely personality recognized by them alone, together with capacity to bring international claims."[1]

The "objective international personality," mentioned by the Court, which transcends the narrow circle of the signatories, is nothing else than an international entity imposed upon the international community by an international settlement. Stipulations in favour of third parties may thus be created irrespective of acceptance by an international settlement.

A second way of achieving the same purpose would seem to be through custom. By Article 3 of the Hay-Pauncefote treaty of 1901,[2] the United States and Great Britain agreed that the Panama Canal should be "free and open to the vessels of commerce and of war of all nations...on terms of entire equality." On the other hand, it is a known fact that the United States wished to avoid bestowing rights of transit on third States.[3] Third parties using the canal are thus enjoying a benefit granted to them by the treaty, but do not have any rights to the use of the canal. However, it may well happen that after a considerable period of time the United States may come to believe that she is bound to allow the free use of the canal, and the nations using it, that they have a right to do so. In that moment the international regime would be established on the Panama Canal through custom, and the international community would be endowed with the right to navigate such an international canal. Nations which had never sent their vessels through it and never accepted any stipulations with regard to it, would now suddenly enjoy the right to traverse it as a result of the new rule of customary law. The initial stipulation of the Hay-Pauncefote treaty in favour of all nations would thus have been transformed into an international right without any ac-

---

[1] *Ibid.*, 1949, p. 185.
[2] 33 *United States Statutes at Large* 2234.
[3] Allen, *Great Britain and The United States*, pp. 601–602.

ceptance having taken place by some, at least, of the members of the international community.

It is safe, then, to conclude, summing up the whole discussion, that an international regime may be established on a canal by consent of the territorial sovereign given in a multilateral treaty, even if the treaty is not universal and in some cases, even if it does not secure acceptance from all the beneficiaries.[1]

After the effects of express consent in its two forms of unilateral declarations and multipartite treaties have been studied in the previous pages, it is time to consider now briefly the influence that the sovereign's tacit consent may have on the establishment of an international regime in canals.

Tacit consent may be given by positive acts, that is, acts implying consent, or by negative acts or sufferance, which means a lack of action, when action is needed if consent is not to be presumed.

The International Court of Justice has recognized both types of tacit consent. In the *Minquiers and Ecrehos* case the Court paid attention, as implying French recognition of British sovereignty over the Minquiers group, to the following two facts[2]: 1) A communication from the French Ambassador to the British Foreign Office "in which the Minquiers were stated to be '*possédés par l'Angleterre*,' and in one of the charts enclosed the Minquiers group was indicated as being British"; 2) a British protest against the construction of a house in Minquiers by a French subject received no response from the French Government but soon afterwards the construction was stopped.

Similarly, the Court mentioned in the decision as a negative act on the part of the French Government, that the British Embassy in a Note of November 12, 1869, to the French Foreign Minister had referred to the Minquiers group as "this dependency of the Channel Islands," and the French Minister in his reply of March 11, 1870, had made no reservation whatsoever in respect of that statement.[3]

It follows from this decision that tacit consent may have on certain occasions the same effects in international law as express con-

---

[1] Another aspect of the problem of International Conventions and Third States, which has not been touched upon in the text is the question of imposing obligations on third States. Guggenheim and a few writers accept its possibility, and the International Court in the *Injuries* case has taken a step in the same direction; but the majority of writers are still averse to that idea, so that the most that can be said today is that international law is evolving in that direction.

[2] I.C.J., *Reports 1953*, p. 71.

[3] *Ibid.*

sent, and, consequently, that there is nothing in its nature that would prevent the territorial sovereign from establishing an international regime in a canal by tacit consent. From a practical viewpoint, however, this way of establishing an international canal presents almost insurmountable difficulties, for tacit consent, except where it would be a question of allowing the growth of a rule of customary law in the sense explained above,[1] would seldom, if ever, be properly evidenced.

(b) *Problems raised when consent is given in a Treaty of Peace*

A treaty of peace, according to international law, has the same binding effect as any other treaty. There seems thus to be no reason for dealing with it now, after it has been proved above that an international canal may be established by treaty. It is a fact, however, that most, if not all, treaties of peace are made under duress, and experience shows that defeated nations take advantage of the first opportunity to get rid of those clauses of the treaty that restraint their freedom of action. These considerations afford sufficient justification for the present study of an international regime established by a treaty of peace.

The treaty of Versailles by its articles 380 to 386 established an international regime in the Kiel canal,[2] which until then had been a purely national canal. According to its provisions, the canal was to be open to all the nations of the world at peace with Germany. The new regime received its first, so to speak, official sanction in the *Wimbledon* case,[3] where the Permanent Court not only upheld the international regime, as part of the treaty of Versailles, but also interpreted its provisions in the most favourable way to the international community.[4]

With the coming to power of *Herr Hitler* there began the gradual undermining of the treaty of Versailles. The suppression of the clauses on demilitarization and rearming was followed on November 14, 1936 by a Proclamation[5] in which the German Government declared that "they no longer recognize as binding the provisions of the Versailles Treaty which concern the German waterways, nor the internationall acts which depend on those provisions..." And in

---

[1] See pp. 34–35 above.
[2] Martens, *N.R.G.*, 3me Ser., v. 11, pp. 636–638.
[3] P.C.I.J., *Ser. A.*, No. 1 (1923).
[4] See the dissenting opinion of Judges Anzilotti and Huber in the same case, especially pp. 38–40.
[5] *Documents 1936*, p. 284.

January of the following year the German Naval High Command issued a Regulation forbidding foreign warships to pass through the Kiel Canal except with authorization obtained beforehand through diplomatic channels.[1]

Whatever the effect of the Proclamation in the absence of any definite response from the signatories of the Treaty of Versailles, the net result was that the Kiel Canal had, for all practical purposes, reverted to the position it held before the treaty of peace of 1919.

After the defeat of Germany in 1945, the situation has become, perhaps, even more confusing, due to the fact that there has been no treaty of peace with Germany yet. In 1950 the German Supreme Court (British Zone) remarked in the *Kiel Canal Collision* case[2] that "whether the Canal has remained an international waterway... seems doubtful because the German Note on German waterways, of November 16, 1936, put an end to internationalization, at least *de facto*, and this step did not meet with any serious resistance on the part of the signatory Powers of the Treaty of Versailles..."

The consideration of the Kiel Canal's history seems to warrant the conclusion that an international regime established in a canal by a treaty of peace will not usually have the same degree of permanency and stability as one established by an ordinary treaty, because the consent given by the territorial sovereign in a treaty of peace is seldom as whole-hearted as when the treaty has been entered into on a basis of complete equality and freedom.

(c) *Problems raised when no consent is given.*

It has been mentioned at the beginning of this section that the consent of the territorial sovereign was absolutely essential for establishing an international regime. There are, however, a number of writers, even today, who base the international regime of canals on principles which are in contradiction to the principle of territorial sovereignty. These principles may be reduced to three: freedom of the seas, international public utility and abuse of rights.

The principle of the freedom of the seas was invoked by some writers in the nineteenth century to defend freedom of navigation in all canals.[3] They were attracted to that way of thinking by the similarity

---

[1] *Ibid.*, p. 286.

[2] Lauterpacht, *Reports 1950*, p. 134.

[3] Calvo, *Le Droit International Théorique et Pratique*, v. 1, p. 507; Holland, *The International Position of the Suez Canal*, p. 277; Fournier de Flaix, *L'Indépendance de l'Egypte et le Régime International du Canal de Suez*, p. 102.

of functions performed by straits and canals; but unfortunately, they overlooked the basic difference that separates them, for canals are artificial waterways, whereas straits are natural. The fact that the canal joins two parts of the open seas cannot obliterate the other fact, that the canal is part of the territory of a State and, thus, subject to the prior principle of territorial sovereignty. This consideration has led modern defenders of this theory to supplement the principle of the freedom of the seas by adding to it one of the other two.

The principle of what may be called international public utility has also been used to justify the imposition of an international regime on canals without the consent of the sovereign. This theory, defended by many writers,[1] has very recently found a strong advocate in the person of a leading French jurist, M. George Scelle.[2] Scelle contends that the unity of the seas and the needs of navigation demand that canals, like straits, be classified as "public domain" so long as this is considered necessary. It follows, to use his own words, that "un Etat qui décide le percement d'un canal sur son territoire, ou qui y consent, consent par la même à l'établissement d'une voie d'eau soumise à la réglementation internationale par son utilisation."[3] The needs of the international community impose themselves *ipso facto* over the principle of territorial sovereignty. This theory, however brilliantly expounded, cannot conceal its basic weakness, that of not being in accord with the facts of actual life. It is, no doubt, a valuable contribution *de lege ferenda*, but under no circumstances could it be considered a *lex lata* today.

The principle of abuse of rights has also been mentioned by another writer[4] in connection with the freedom of the seas, as demanding an international regime in canals independently of consent. The principle itself has been recognized by the Permanent Court,[5] by Arbitral Tribunals,[6] and, most recently, by the international Law Commission,[7] but its application to the regime of canals is unwarranted, for

---

[1] Pradier–Fodéré, *Traité de Droit International Public*, v. 2, p. 204; Moussa, *Essai sur le Canal de Suez*, p. 134; Fauchille, *Traité de Droit International Public*, t. 1, 2me part., pp. 291–2.

[2] Scelle, *La Nationalisation du Canal de Suez et le Droit International*, (*A.F.D.I.*, 2 (1956) 3–19).

[3] *Ibid.*, p. 7.

[4] Quintano Ripolles, *El Canal de Suez*, pp. 76–77.

[5] P.C.I.J., *Ser. A*, No. 7 (1926), p. 30 and No. 24 (1930), p. 12; *Ser. A/B*, No. 46 (1932), p. 167.

[6] *Annual Digest 1938–1940*, Case No. 104: *Trail Smelter Arbitration* (U.S. v. Canada), p. 317.

[7] *Report of the International Law Commission*, 5th Sess., U.N. Gen. Ass., *Doc. A/2456*, para. 100.

the concept of abuse of rights involves always an element of ar-
bitrariness and of unlawfulness[1] which are lacking in the present case.
As international law stands today, each state is the sole judge of
what policies are advantageous to itself.

At the end of this rather long section, it may be convenient by way
of summary to draw the conclusions that follow from our inquiry:

1) An international canal is a canal subject to an international
regime.

2) An international regime may be established on a canal only by
consent of the territorial sovereign.

3) That consent may be given in a unilateral declaration followed
by acceptance by the international community.

4) The same consent may also be given in a multilateral treaty,
either signed by all states or by some only.

5) If the treaty has been concluded among some States only, the
international regime stipulated in it may be extended later to non-
signatories either by their express or tacit consent to it, or, even
without their consent, by application, in some cases, of the doctrine
of international settlements or, in some other cases, through custom.

6) Consent given by the sovereign in a treaty of peace has the same
legal effects as that given in any other treaty, but, in practice, the
international regime so established may have less stability.

7) Principles adduced by some writers to supplant the need of
consent of the territorial sovereign in establishing an international
regime, are shown upon analysis to have no validity for that purpose.

Section III   LEGAL NATURE

Generally speaking, international canals may be said to be connected with the related field of international rivers and international
straits, and, it may also be surmised, that their legal nature partakes
of some of the characteristics of the latter. The present section will
be devoted to a more thorough examination of that relationship.

A river by its very nature is part of the territory over which it
flows and subject to the sovereignty of the State to which that
territory belongs. International rivers are no exception to this rule,
but, unlike national rivers, they connect more than one State with

---

[1] See Oppenheim–Lauterpacht, *International Law*, v. 1 (8th ed.), p. 345; Guggenheim, *Traité de Droit international public*, v. 1, p. 91.

the open sea.[1] They thus perform a function which goes beyond the purely national interest of any one State, and consequently, their concept involves an international element which is wholly lacking in the case of national rivers.

This element, in the opinion of the Permanent Court as described in the case of the *International Commission of the Oder*, is to be sought not "in the idea of a right of passage in favor of upstream States, but in that of a community of interest of riparian states," which in turn "becomes the basis of a common legal right, the essential features of which are the perfect equality of all riparian States in the use of the whole course of the river, and the exclusion of any preferential privilege of any one riparian State in relation to the others."[2]

As far as navigation of the river was concerned, the legal system, which was originally devised in favor of riparian States, was later extended, partly by conventional law[3] and partly by customary law, to the whole international community. All nations of the world were supposed to have a right to navigate international rivers. Freedom of navigation, however, could not override the principle of territorial sovereignty based, as it was, on the inescapable fact that the river is always a part of the territory. That freedom, therefore, could in no case be absolute; only merchant vessels have a right to navigate international rivers, and even this, subject to many conditions. Thus, of the two principles that play an important role in the concept of international rivers, territorial sovereignty may be said to occupy a pre-eminent position; freedom of navigation, a rather subordinate one.

International straits, on the other hand, when they connect two open seas, are necessarily part of those seas and subject to their regime. Freedom of navigation in straits is only a corollary to the freedom of the seas. The very concept of a strait, however, presupposes that its waters wash the shores of one or more States. If the strait is very narrow, all of its waters belong to the territorial sea of the State or States that own its shores; if the straigt is wide enough, part at least of its waters will be classified as territorial. Straits, therefore, are also subject, at least in part, to the principle of territorial sovereignty.

---

[1] See above, ch. II, sect. I.

[2] P.C.I.J., *Ser. A*, No. 23 (1929), p.27.

[3] See Congress of Vienna, Art. 109; Congress of Paris (1856), Art. 15; Treaty of Versailles, Art. 332; Barcelona Convention on Navigable Waterways, Art. 3. For full references, see above p. 1, notes 1, to 4.

Hence, the same conflict between freedom of navigation, as the international element, and territorial sovereignty, as the national element, that has been found in the case of international rivers. In this conflict, as it developed through history, the international element has been steadily gaining ground until it was recognized by the International Court as being the more important of the two.

In the *Corfu Channel* case not only did the Court accept freedom of navigation for merchant vessels, but it declared to be "in accordance with international custom that States in time of peace have a right to send their warships through straits...without the previous authorization of a coastal State, provided that the passage is *innocent*."[1] The significance of the principle of freedom was emphasized again by the Court when it stated that even in the extraordinary circumstances in which Albania found herself at the time, being technically in a state of war with Greece, she "would have been justified in issuing regulations in respect of the passage of warships through the Strait [Corfu], but not in prohibiting such passage or in subjecting it to the requirement of special authorization."[2]

Although territorial sovereignty is fundamentally preserved in the regime of international straits, freedom of navigation holds the first place, as immediately derived from the freedom of the seas. The principles that play a role in international straits are therefore basically the same as in international rivers, but their relative positions have been reversed.

Differing from international rivers and international straits, though related to both as occupying a middle position between them, international canals have a status of their own in international law. Being artificially constructed, the regime to which a canal is subject depends entirely on the territorial sovereign. His consent is essentially required in order to have an international canal. This consideration would seem to put a heavy emphasis, even after consent has been given for establishing an international regime, on the principle of sovereignty. In this respect, international canals show a marked similarity to international rivers.

On the other hand, a canal, once it has been dedicated to the use of the world, that is, once it has been made international, performs a function closely resembling that of international straits, in that it joins two parts of the open seas, over which the principle of absolute

[1] I.C.J., *Reports 1949*, p. 28.
[2] *Ibid.*, p. 29.

freedom of navigation prevails. From this viewpoint, international canals have much in common with international straits.

If similarities among the three waterways are many, dissimilarities at the same time are not lacking. After dedication of the canal to international navigation, territorial sovereignty over it remains permanently more restricted than in the case of international rivers, for the greater interest of the international community in navigating the former.

On the other hand, freedom of navigation in canals is never a corollary to the freedom of the seas, as in international straits. That freedom is subject not only to the conditions which the sovereign may have attached to the granting of his consent, but also to all the other restrictions that flow from territorial sovereignty and are not incompatible with the bare principle of freedom of navigation, such as specific regulations required by the nature of the canal or by the security of the state. Freedom of navigation in canals is thus more restricted than in straits.

From the double point of view of similarities and dissimilarities just described, it may be seen that international canals occupy a middle position between the other two waterways, being less subject to the domineering influence of territorial sovereignty than international rivers, but at the same time having a far greater control over navigation than is the case with international straits.

Turning now from the governing principles to the true legal nature of international canals, this may be said to be nothing else than a voluntarily accepted permanent limitation of sovereignty whereby freedom of navigation through the canal is internationally guaranteed to all nations.

The limitation of sovereignty spoken of was characterized by the German Supreme Court (British Zone) in the *Kiel Canal Collision* case[1] as "a kind of State servitude in so far as the freedom of navigation requires the same," and would seem therefore to pertain to the category of those rights which are attached to the territory to which they refer independently of its actual or potential sovereign, and which are usually known in legal parlance as "real" or "territorial" rights, among which the so-called international servitudes belong. This right, in the case of international canals, stems directly from an international transaction, or an international act of a contractual nature, which, as has been explained above, may be either a unilat-

[1] Lauterpacht, *Reports 1950*, p. 134.

eral declaration accepted by the international community, or simply a multilateral treaty.

No undue significance, however, should be attached to this interpretation. The international transaction, which is at the basis of the "real" right, may be sufficient explanation in itself for that permanent limitation of sovereignty, in which the legal nature of an international canal essentially consists, as the Permanent Court stated in the *Wimbledon* case:

> "Whether the German Government is bound by virtue of a servitude or by virtue of a contractual obligation...to allow free access to the Kiel Canal... the fact remains that Germany has to submit to an important limitation of the exercise of the sovereign rights..."[1]

Section IV   LEGAL CONSEQUENCES

From the fact of having had a canal placed under an international regime there follow certain legal consequences which must be examined in turn. The first consequence is a real limitation of territorial sovereignty. This belongs to the very essence of an international canal, as it has been expounded in the preceding section. The limitation, however, is not absolute, but "suffered only within the framework of the true purpose of internationalization, i. e. general freedom of navigation," as the German Supreme Court put it in the *Collision* case mentioned above.[2] It follows that in all other respects the sovereignty of the State remains unimpaired, particularly its "power of jurisdiction and the field of application of the local system of law."[3]

The preceding statement would seem to show not only that the bottom of the canal belongs to the State which owns the shores as part of its territory, but that even its waters come under the exclusive jurisdiction of the Government, and are, consequently, to be considered as national or internal waters. The fact that the territorial sovereign is bound to allow freedom of navigation in the canal – the only requirement implied in the international regime – could not possibly change the legal nature of its waters which had always been national before, as a treaty providing for a right of transit across the

---

[1] P.C.I.J., *Ser. A*, No. 1 (1923), p. 24. For a different concept of servitude from the one expressed in the text, see the recent monograph by Vali, *Servitudes of International Law*, pp. 309–312.

[2] Lauterpacht, *Reports 1950*, p. 134.

[3] *Ibid.*

territory of another State could not by itself make that territory any less national than it had been before the treaty was concluded.

The second consequence that follows from an international canal is freedom of navigation for all nations. It may be convenient for the sake of clarity to deal separately with merchant vessels and with warships.

A. *Merchant Vessels*: The nature of an international canal demands that the canal be open to all merchant vessels at least in time of peace. If the canal is not open to all merchant vessels without exception – something which the territorial sovereign is perfectly entitled to do – there may be a national canal; but according to the definition given by the Permanent Court in the *Wimbledon* case[1] there will never be an international canal.

Such freedom of navigation, however, as described, applies only in time of peace. In time of war, regulations issued by the territorial sovereign and even the exclusion of some merchant vessels, when their transit may compromise the neutrality or the security of the State, would not seem to go against the essence of an international canal. It is true that the Permanent Court held the opposite opinion in the *Wimbledon* case with regard to the Kiel Canal,[2] but it must be remembered that the Court was at the time interpreting the meaning of some articles of the Treaty of Versailles. In the absence of any treaty, the illuminating remarks, made by Judges Anzilotti and Huber in their dissenting opinion[3] to the effect that the obligation undertaken by a State to maintain a canal free and open does not exclude its right to take the measures necessary to protect its interests as a belligerent or neutral power, should be accepted as self-evident. To them may be added Article 15 of the *Barcelona Statute on Navigable Waterways*,[4] which expressly states that the Statute "does not prescribe the rights and duties of belligerents and neutrals in time of war." The same conclusion seems to follow from the decision of the Mixed Court of Appeal of Egypt in the case of *Egypt v. The British India Navigation Co.*, in which the Court held that a Government is not infringing any acquired right in prohibiting foreigners, in the interests of its own security, from engaging and transporting arms over its territory to a neighbouring State.[5]

---

[1] See above, p. 25.
[2] P.C.I.J., *Ser. A*, No. 1 (1923), p. 28.
[3] *Ibid.*, p. 40. See also *Ibid.*, pp. 38–39.
[4] L.N.T.S., 7 (1921–1922) 35.
[5] *Annual Digest 1927–1928*, p. 28.

For all these reasons, it would seem that the obligation to maintain an international canal free and open to merchant vessels of all nations applies in all its rigour to the time of peace only, and that in time of war the territorial sovereign would be justified in taking those measures which he deems necessary to protect its neutrality or its security.

B. *Warships*: By analogy to the regime prevailing in international rivers it may be said that a State which owns an international canal is not bound to grant freedom of navigation to warships even in time of peace. Article 17 of the *Barcelona Statute on Navigable Waterways* provides,

"In the absence of any agreement to the contrary...this Statute has no reference to the navigation of vessels of war...or in general (to vessels) exercising any kind of public authority."[1]

The conclusion seems to be that the passage of warships through an international canal in time of peace is at the discretion of the territorial sovereign. In time of war, however, and in the absence of a general treaty, the rules of neutrality demand that the canal be closed to the warships of belligerents.

The third legal consequence that follows from an international canal is that the regime of freedom established in it must be maintained permanently. The concept of permanency does not by any means imply that the regime of the canal should be unchangeable but only, as the Permanent Court remarked in the *Wimbledon* case,[2] that it should be internationally guaranteed, so that it would not be open to the territorial sovereign to modify it at will. If any changes are required, they should be made in accord with the international community, which acquired certain rights when the regime was first established in the canal.

The same requirement of permanency would also prevent the territorial sovereign, after he has agreed to the establishment of an international regime, from making new continuous demands upon the users of the canal which, though small in themselves, may amount in the course of time to a real change of the existing regime. Such would be the case if tolls in the canal were progressively raised to such an extent that navigation through it would become practically impossible.

[1] L.N.T.S., 7 (1921–1922) 35.
[2] P.C.I.J., *Ser. A*, No. 1 (1923), p. 22. See also above, p. 38.

The three consequences just mentioned are those that follow inevitably from the nature of an international canal as it has been defined above, in accordance, it is believed, with the decisions of international courts. The territorial sovereign is, of course, always free to restrict still further his exclusive rights over the canal and to grant by treaty further concessions to the international community. But the regime of an international canal as such should always be distinguished from those other possible regimes which may be superimposed over it by treaty. In order to avoid confusion, it is submitted to give to the special regime of international canals the name of "regime of internationality," by which is meant the legal status of a canal in which there is internationally guaranteed freedom of navigation in time of peace for the merchant vessels of all nations.

The regime so defined has to be sharply distinguished from the following related ones:

1) *Regime of internationalization*: Traditionally,under the name of internationalization, two concepts have been included: first, what has been described above as "regime of internationality"; and second, what may be termed international administration. That there is a difference between these two regimes was already recognized by the Permanent Court in the case of the *International Commission of the Oder*.[1] It is now proposed to reserve the name of *internationalization* exclusively for a regime of international administration, by analogy to municipal law, where an enterprise is said to be nationalized if its ownership, or its administration, or both, are in the hands of the State. By the same token, a regime of internationalization of canals would imply an international administration of those canals by the United Nations or by an international commission. It is clear that such a regime could only be established by treaty.

2) *Regime of demilitarization*: "Demilitarization denotes the agreement of two or more States by treaty not to fortify, or station troops upon, a particular zone or territory."[2] There is nothing to prevent the territorial sovereign from demilitarizing the canal by treaty, in addition to making it international, if he so wishes, but this is not implied in or required by the international regime.

3) *Regime of neutralization*: Neutralization of a territory, as distinct from that of a state, "denotes the exclusion by treaty of a particular part of the territory of a State from the region of war, so

---

[1] P.C.I.J., *Ser. A*, No. 23 (1929), p. 23.
[2] Oppenheim–Lauterpacht, *International Law*, v. 2 (7th ed.), p. 244, n. 1.

that warlike preparations or operations become illegal thereon."[1] A permanent neutralization of territory would always require a general treaty of the Powers. It is not open to doubt that, without such a treaty freely entered into by the territorial sovereign, a canal could not possibly be neutralized, for it would impose obligations on other Powers without their consent.

[1] *Ibid.*

CHAPTER III

THE SUEZ CANAL FROM 1854 TO 1888:
THE INTERNATIONAL CANAL

At the end of the first chapter, the question, left unanswered, was whether the Suez Canal was an international canal. It seems clear now, after what has been said in the preceding chapter, that an international canal is a canal subject to a regime of internationality. On the other hand, there is no doubt that the Constantinople Convention of 1888 purported to establish an international regime in the Suez Canal. The question remains, however, as to the status of the canal before that Convention took place. It is the purpose of the present chapter to inquire into the legal status of the Suez Canal between 1854 and 1888.

The British Prize Court for Egypt at the beginning of the first World War categorically denied any international character to the Canal during that period. In the *Gutenfels* case, the Court said that

"...the construction of the Canal had nothing international about it. It was a purely commercial bargain made between the Egyptian Government and the Canal company, and subsequently ratified by the Sultan of Turkey... There is nothing in these agreements that can possibly give rights to third parties. The Government and the company between them are at perfect liberty to vary their contracts so as to exclude or prefer the ship of any nationality..."[1]

The same opinion is held by a number of writers for whom the Concessions and the Sultan's *Firman* are nothing but acts of internal government that do not give rise to any international obligations on the part of the Egyptian and Turkish Governments. "The passage of ships was not a right but a privilege granted by the Ottoman Empire to other nations."[2]

A second opinion expounded by P. Visscher accepts the possibility of creating international rights by a unilateral declaration, but contends that in the case of the Suez Canal a limitation of sovereignty

---

[1] *B.C. Prize Cases*, pp. 108–109.
[2] Avram, *The Evolution of the Suez Canal Status from 1869 up to 1956*, p. 31. See also Whittuck, *International Canals*, pp. 8–9, and Badawi, *Le Statut International du Canal de Suez*, (Festschrift für Jean Spiropoulos, pp. 13–14).

cannot lightly be inferred from the terms of the concessions.[1]

A third opinion is held by Fauchille who maintains that all the States acquired, by the Concessions, a right to use the canal vis - à - vis the territorial sovereign, but that owing to the unilateral character of the declaration, the regime thus established does not offer the same guarantees for the users of the canal as if it had been the result of a mutual undertaking.[2]

As against this background of opinion, the present inquiry is based on certain fundamental premises which have been dealt with in the previous chapter and must always be kept in mind. If rights of other States are mentioned, these rights have necessarily been granted by the territorial sovereign. The point at issue is not whether these rights need be granted, but whether they have been granted or not. Neither is it a question as to whether the rights must necessarily be granted in a bilateral convention or not, for it has been proved that a unilateral declaration, specially if followed by acceptance, is sufficient to create international rights; nor is it a question of the external form of the declaration or of the acceptance, for it has also been shown in the same chapter that the declaration may be enshrined even in a municipal law or decree, provided the intention of the sovereign is clearly manifested, and that a tacit acceptance by conduct or otherwise may have the same effects as an express one.

The object of the inquiry is thus limited to the following two points: first, it must be ascertained whether the territorial sovereign at the time of the Concessions for the construction of the Canal had any intention of granting rights of transit over it to other States, which were accepted by them; second, in case of an affirmative reply to the first question, it must be further ascertained whether the rights thus granted amounted to the establishment of a regime of internationality in the canal. If the answer to the second question is also in the affirmative, it will follow that the Suez Canal was an international canal from the very beginning of its existence.

Section I   THE INTENTION OF THE SOVEREIGN

On November 15, 1854, Ferdinand de Lesseps spoke for the first time to the Viceroy of Egypt about his project for opening the Suez

[1] P. Visscher, *Les Aspects Juridiques Fondamentaux de la Question de Suez*, (R.G. D.I.P., 3me ser., 29 (1958) 405).

[2] Fauchille, *Traité de Droit International Public*, t. 1, 2me part., pp. 316–317.

Canal; the project was immediately accepted.[1] Ten days later, on the occasion of a general gathering of all foreign consuls at Cairo, who had come to his palace to compliment him, the Viceroy publicly and purposely announced to them his intention of constructing a canal and of granting the right to execute and exploit the undertaking to a company composed of investors of all nations.[2] On November 27, the Viceroy instructed de Lesseps to contact the British Consul General in Egypt; in his letter, de Lesseps pointed out that

"Son Altesse…m'a engagé à vous communiquer la copie du mémoire qu'elle m'a demandé sur cette question, [the opening of the canal], dans laquelle elle a le désir de satisfaire les intérêts de l'Angleterre comme ceux des autres nations…"[3]

The first Concession to de Lesseps, granted on November 30, provided in its Article 6,

"The rates of the transit charges of the Suez Canal, arranged between the company and the Viceroy of Egypt and collected by the agents of the company, shall always be the same for all nations; no special advantage may ever be stipulated for the exclusive benefit of any of them."[4]

On December 2, copies of the Concession and of all pertinent documents were forwarded to all foreign consuls by de Lesseps upon the advice of the sovereign.[5] In a letter of January 1855 to the Emperor Napoleon III, the Viceroy of Egypt, after telling him of his project for opening the Canal, added the following paragraph:

"J'ose espérer, sire, que Votre Majesté…daignera donner son approbation à un projet dont la réalisation ouvrirait un nouveau débouché au commerce et à l'industrie de toutes les nations de l'Europe."[6]

The facts and documents just quoted are all pointing to a certain aim. If it is not possible to construe them as implying a renunciation of sovereignty in favor of other States, they at least show, without a doubt, the Viceroy's intention to open the canal for the benefit of all nations and even to act at all times in accord with them. If there were at this stage no official negotiations with other nations, this was due not so much to any desire of avoiding international commitments as to the fear that interminable discussions might delay the execution of the project.[7]

---

[1] Lesseps, *Lettres*, v. 1, p. 20.
[2] *Ibid.*, v. 1, pp. 39–40.
[3] *Ibid.*, v. 1, p. 45.
[4] *The Suez Problem*, p. 1.
[5] Lesseps, *Lettres*, v. 1, p. 51.
[6] *Ibid.*, v. 1, p. 88.
[7] See Lesseps's letter of October 28, 1855, to the Secretary of the Treasury at Vienna, Baron de Bruck. *Ibid.*, v. 1, pp. 267–268.

On January 5, 1856, the Viceroy granted Lesseps the second Concession, which clarified and, for all purposes, supplanted the one of 1854. Article 14 of this important instrument read,

"We solemnly declare, for ourselves and our successors, subject to ratification by His Imperial Majesty the Sultan, that the great maritime canal from Suez to Pelusium and the ports belonging to it shall be open forever, as neutral passages, to every merchant vessel crossing from one sea to the other, without any distinction, exclusion, or preference with respect to persons or nationalities, in consideration of the payment of the fees, and compliance with the regulations established by the universal company, the concession–holder, for the use of the said canal and its appurtenances."[1]

The purpose of this most controversial Article cannot exclusively or even primarily be to assure the Company that the canal would always remain open. The solemnity of the declaration, which resembles in its form a binding international commitment, and, above all, the express reference to a permanent regime – open forever, *ouvert à toujours* – whereas the company, according to Article 16, had its life limit fixed at 99 years, inescapably shows that what the Viceroy had here mostly in view was the international community, and that by this Article he was addressing himself to each and every one of the nations of the world. The Article is thus in the nature of a true unilateral declaration. From its terms alone, however, it is not possible to determine whether this is a declaration by which international rights are granted to other States, or only a mere declaration of policy from which no binding international effects follow. In order to settle this point, it is necessary to have recourse again to the actual conduct of the parties involved.

Th Viceroy of Egypt, however, was not at that time the full sovereign of the country, but was subject to the suzerainty of the Ottoman Empire. Any international engagement to which Egypt was a party had to be ratified by the Sultan of Turkey, and this applied particularly to the concessions for the construction of the Suez Canal. The intention of the Sultan, therefore, as the ultimate authority in this matter, must unavoidably be ascertained in all the negotiations that took place regarding the canal.

Writing in December 1858 to the Viceroy of Egypt the Grand-Vizier of Turkey remarked:

"Votre Altesse a trop de perspicacité pour qu'il soit nécessaire de lui expliquer que le percement de l'isthme étant une affaire très considérable, *tant au point de vue international*[2] que sous le rapport gouvernemental...il est de toute

[1] See Appendix A, below.
[2] Italics mine.

nécessité...de peser avec exactitude les avantages et les désavantages qui peuvent en résulter, *tant pour les diverses puissances*, que pour...l'Egypte."[1]

On September 2, 1859, Lesseps explained to the Viceroy of Egypt the reasons for the delay in obtaining the ratification of the concessions in the following significant words:

"La Sublime Porte...attend que les puissances étrangères se soient mises d'accord entre elles sur les questions concernant l'usage universel du nouveau passage maritime. En un mot, c'est une négociation internationale qu'elle désire."[2]

On January 4, 1860, the Ottoman Government sent an identical Despatch to London and Paris stating the essential conditions required for the solution of the Canal question. Of these, the third was

"...the guarantees to be asked and obtained from the Great Maritime Powers, guarantees which must be accepted by all the High Powers, allies of the Sublime Porte, so as to secure the Government of the Sultan against the consequences of any conflict between these Powers, and to give to the navigation of the Canal a security based on the particular interests of Turkey, and on the general interests of Europe."[3]

And on April 6, 1863, the same point of view was reiterated in a further and more forceful note to the same capitals. It may be convenient to quote at some length from it:

"...when some years ago the Sublime Porte was informed of the Suez Canal question it reserved to itself the power of imposing its conditions on the other parties to the draft scheme which was submitted to it, and declared that it desired to see a previous understanding established between the two greatest Maritime Powers with regard to the external guarantees which the opening of so important a channel would demand... It does not enter into the mind of the Sublime Porte to wish to prevent the realization of an undertaking which might be one of general utility. But it cannot consent to it (1) except with the certainty of obtaining international stipulations which, as in the case of the Straits of the Dardanelles and the Bosphorus, would guarantee absolute neutrality..."[4]

What this neutrality implied in the mind of the Ottoman Government is shown in a Vizierial letter of August 1, 1863, to the French Embassy at Constantinople, in which one of the conditions required for the opening of the Canal is phrased thus: "Des garanties suffisantes que le Canal serait exclusivement destiné au commerce." In the same letter, the following paragraph may be found:

---

[1] Lesseps, *Lettres*, v. 3, p. 158.
[2] *Ibid.*, v. 3, p. 208.
[3] *Parl. Pap.*, Egypt No. 20 (1883), C.3734, pp. 6–7.
[4] *Ibid.*, p. 4.

"Ainsi, dès que les questions [the other conditions mentioned]...auront reçu, *par rapport à l'intérieur*, une solution conforme à ce qui précède, il sera alors procédé, *par rapport à l'extérieur*, à la negociation des conventions, qui auront pour objet la destination exclusive du canal maritime à la marine marchande en général."[1]

From the brief sketch of the negotiations just described, the general attitude of the Porte toward the Suez Canal question may easily be gathered. When the project first came to its attention, the Ottoman Government not only did not reject it or reserve the future use of the canal for its own benefit in the manner of a national canal, as it was undoubtedly entitled to do, but on the contrary it declared itself ready to allow the construction of the canal as an "undertaking of general utility," provided certain conditions were fulfilled. Of these, some referred to private agreements between the Viceroy and the Company, qualified by the Sublime Porte as "*par rapport à l'intérieur*," whereas others, the so-called "*par rapport à l'extérieur*," were concerned with "the guarantees to be obtained from the Powers" in the form of "international stipulations," so as to secure the "absolute neutrality" of the canal. If these expressions mean anything, they must necessarily imply the intention of the sovereign of entering into international engagements with other nations for the purpose of securing to merchant vessels the free navigation in the canal. Such an intention implies, in turn, a renunciation of sovereignty in favor of other States to whom rights of transit are granted, which cannot be revoked except with their consent.

The first group of conditions, *par rapport à l'interieur*, were fulfilled by the Agreement of February 22, 1866, between the Viceroy and the Company, which expressly included and approved all the former concessions and agreements.[2] The Sultan then gave his official consent to the construction of the canal by a *Firman* of March 19 of the same year, which incorporated *in toto* the Agreement of February 22, and referred "to the acts and agreements included and set forth therein, which form the complete agreement."[3] Thus, by the granting of this *Firman*, the Sultan of Turkey made the Viceroy's concessions his own, and gave unqualified approval to all and each of the provisions contained in them.

The second group of conditions, *par rapport à l'extérieur*, that is to say, the "international stipulations" that were designed to bring

[1] Lesseps, *Lettres*, v. 4, pp. 317–318.
[2] *B.F.St. Pap.*, 56 (1865–1866) 277. English trans. in *The Suez Problem*, p. 9.
[3] *B.F.St.Pap.*, 56 (1865–1866) 294. English trans. in The Society of Compar. Legis. and Int. Law, *The Suez Canal*, p. 41.

formally into operation the guarantees for the neutrality of the canal, did not materialize until the Constantinople Convention of 1888. As a result, the only legal instrument guaranteeing freedom of navigation in the canal at the time of its inauguration in 1869, was Article 14 of the 1856 Concession, which had been expressly included and approved in the Sultan's *Firman*, as explained above. Was, then, this Article a truly unilateral declaration by which international rights were granted to other nations, or must it be considered as a mere declaration of policy without any legal effects?

The answer does not seem to be open to doubt. The lengthy negotiations, referred to above, between the Ottoman Government and the Governments of other States, have shown beyond peradventure the Sultan's intention of concluding international conventions that would guarantee absolute freedom of navigation in the canal to merchant vessels. The Sultan, therefore, was willing and ready to give up part of his sovereign rights over the future canal and to transfer them to other nations for the benefit of all. Now, when he decided to grant the *Firman* and with it accepted the 1856 Concession, he *ipso facto* also accepted the declaration of Article 14 and gave to it its full meaning, which was so much in accord with his intention at the time.

On the other hand, the promulgation of the Sultan's *Firman* was an indication that the differences between Great Britain and France with regard to the canal, which were at the bottom of the Sultan's insistence for formal guarantees of its neutrality, had successfully been overcome. The easing of tensions that ensued made the question of formal guarantees much less imperative than before. The Sultan knew now that he could count upon the goodwill and enlightened self-interest of the Powers to preserve the neutrality of the canal, and the Great Powers were assured of the Sultan's definite intention to maintain the canal free and open forever to the vessels of all nations. There was thus established a tacit understanding between both parties, whereby the rights granted by the Sultan and so clearly expressed in the declaration of Article 14 were quietly accepted by the other States. When at long last the canal was inaugurated in 1869 and traffic began to flow in both directions, no government made any request for a formal convention, for everyone of them knew exactly where it stood with regard to the canal. And there the matter lay for a number of years, and might have lain even longer had not the British occupation of Egypt made the Constantinople Convention of 1888 a practical necessity.

The conclusions presently arrived at with respect to the Sultan's intention are further strengthened by the conduct of the parties on subsequent occasions. On January 1, 1873, the Ottoman Government invited all the Great Powers to establish a commission which would determine the rules for measuring the tonnage of all vessels passing through the canal and fix the tolls to be exacted from them.[1] This move on the part of Turkey provoked an official reply of January 9 from the French Foreign Minister to the Embassy at Constantinople, in which the following paragraph may be read:

> "Elle [the Porte] comprend, en effet, que le caractère essentiellement international de la grande voie qu'elle a ouverte aux marines de tous les pays lui impose l'obligation morale de ne pas aggraver les conditions de ce transit sans un accord préalable avec les Gouvernements intéressés."[2]

In order to deal with the problems mentioned in the Turkish Circular of January 1st, a Conference was held at Constantinople at the end of 1873. In its session of December 13, the Ottoman Delegate made the following declaration to the assembled representatives:

> "It is understood that no modification, for the future, of the conditions for the passage through the Canal shall be permitted, whether in regard to the navigation toll or the dues for towage, anchorage, pilotage, etc., except with the consent of the Sublime Porte, which will not take any decision on this subject without previously coming to an understanding with the principal Powers interested therein."[3]

The declaration was inserted *verbatim* in the Final Report of the Conference, which was "unanimously adopted" at its last session,[4] and thus became the standard norm accepted by all for the handling in the future of all problems connected with the canal. It is indisputable that the declaration represents a substantial limitation of the Ottoman Government's freedom of action in the canal, and, consequently, that it implies an important renunciation of sovereignty. It is hard, however, to believe that the Sultan of Turkey was willing to give the Powers a share in the management of the Canal if he had previously refused to give them even a right of transit through it. Nor is it easy to understand what the Powers might have expected to gain from such an arrangement if the Canal may at any time and without their previous consent be closed to the vessels of any or all nations. The conclusion, then, seems inescapable that the

---

[1] *Doc. Dipl.*, Affaire du Canal de Suez (1881), pp. 22–23.
[2] *Ibid.*, p. 25.
[3] *Parl. Pap.*, Commercial No. 19 (1874), C.1075, p. 319.
[4] *Ibid.*, Annexe 1, p. 331.

express granting of rights to the Powers, made by the declaration of the Ottoman Government, presupposes former rights of transit, enjoyed by the international community, to which the new ones are now spontaneously added by the Sublime Porte.

As a result of the declaration, matters concerning the Canal began to be handled in common by the representatives of the Powers. When in 1876, after the purchase of the shares by the British Government, Colonel Stokes concluded his agreement with de Lesseps,[1] the Prime Minister of Great Britain sent a copy of it to all the participants of the 1873 Conference with the following proviso: "It is entirely provisional, and subject to the assent of the Powers whom the Sublime Porte undertook to consult before consenting to any modification of the Suez Canal dues."[2] To which the Porte answered in a Circular Note to the Foreign Representatives at Constantinople:

"La Sublime Porte sanctionnera les modifications proposées, par MM. de Lesseps et Stokes, si elles sont agréées par le Gouvernement de...et par les autres Puissances Maritimes qui ont été representées dans la Commission de 1873."[3]

The same procedure was followed in the question of new rules for tonnage measurement in 1878,[4] and again when the Canal was put in jeopardy by Arabi's rebellion in 1882.[5] Even after the British had been in occupation of Egypt for over a year, Mr. Gladstone could still tell the House of Commons on July 23, 1883,

"I wish to announce that we cannot undertake to do any act inconsistent with the acknowledgement...that the canal has been made for the benefit of all nations at large, and that the rights connected with it are matters of common European interest."[6]

Thus, the history of the Canal subsequent to its inauguration supports the contention expounded above, that the territorial sovereign, represented ultimately by the Sultan of Turkey, had from the beginning granted to other States certain rights over the Canal, thereby voluntarily accepting a partial though permanent limitation of its sovereignty. It now remains to consider whether the rights so

---

[1] By this Agreement the British Government was given ten votes in the General Assembly of shareholders and the right to appoint three representatives to the Board of Directors. *Parl. Pap.*, Egypt No. 9 (1876), C,1525.

[2] *Ibid.*, p. 29.

[3] *Ibid.*, Commercial No. 14 (1877), C.1797, p. 31.

[4] *Ibid.*, Commercial No. 12 (1878), C.2010, p. 82, and Commercial No. 23 (1879), C.2399, p. 67.

[5] *Ibid.*, Egypt No. 17 (1882), C.3391, Inclosure in No. 462.

[6] 282 *Parl. Deb.* (3rd ser.) 152 (1883).

granted amounted in fact to the establishment of a regime of internationality in the Canal.

Section II   THE REGIME OF INTERNATIONALITY

The regime of internationality of canals has been defined above
as "the legal status of a canal in which there is internationally
guaranteed freedom of navigation in time of peace for the merchant
vessels of all nations."[1]

The status of the Suez Canal with regard to the international
community was contained in the concessions and agreements ratified
by the Sultan of Turkey and tacitly accepted by the nations of the
world. By Article 6 of the first Concession, later reaffirmed in Article
15 of the second one, all nations are promised equality of transit
charges and equality of treatment in the Canal.[2] Article 14 of the
1856 Concession contained the solemn declaration mentioned above,[3]
whereby the territorial sovereign pledged himself to maintain the
canal open forever, as a neutral passage, to every merchant vessel
crossing it. Article 10 of the Convention of February 22, 1866,
reserved to the Egyptian Government the right to occupy any strategic point in the Canal area necessary for the defense of the country,
but it immediately added the proviso that "such an occupation shall
not be a bar to navigation and shall respect the servitudes attaching
to the free-boards of the canal."[4] Lastly, by Article 13 of the same
Convention, the sovereign exempted from all duties "the general
transit through the canal of the vessels of all nations."[5]

According to these documents, the Canal was to be open to the
merchant vessels of all nations. It was to be open not only in time of
peace but even in time of war, for it is hard to see what other meaning
the expression "neutral passage" may have in that context,[6] although,
as explained above, this concession on the part of Turkey was to
be matched by the guarantees given by the Powers. The regime thus

[1] See above, p. 46.
[2] See above, p. 50.
[3] See above, p. 51.
[4] See above, p. 53, n. 2.
[5] *Ibid.*
[6] The Egyptian writer Badawi in the article mentioned above (p. 48, n. 2) maintains that in the Concessions and Firman "le temps de guerre n'est nullement
envisagé" (p. 13); no proof, however, is offered in support of this interpretation which
runs counter to the letter of Article 14 of the 1856 Concession and to the lengthy
negotiations on the neutrality of the canal referred to in Section 1 of this chapter.

established, as far as the Sultan was concerned, goes even further than what is strictly required by a regime of internationality. The only point that might conceivably have been open to question in the preceding documents – the international guarantees, essentially required in a regime of internationality – has already been disposed of in the previous section, where it has been shown how the sovereign's intention of granting rights of transit was followed by the tacit acceptance of the Powers. The regime, then, to which the Suez Canal was subject from the beginning fulfills all the conditions required by a regime of internationality.

Very soon, however, with the acquiescence of the sovereign new usages were introduced, which had not been included in the original set of rights already granted by the international regime. Thus, during the Franco-German War of 1870 the canal remained open to the merchant vessels of all nations, including those of the belligerents.[1] At the Constantinople Conference of 1873, the rule was officially established that vessels of war were to have in the future the right to pass through the canal, although this had been purposely excluded by the Sultan from all the Concessions.[2] At the time of the Russo-Turkish War in 1877, the canal not only remained open to the merchant vessels of the belligerents but even to their warships, Great Britain serving notice to both parties that any attempt to blockade or otherwise to interfere with the canal or its approaches would be regarded by the British Government as a grave injury to the commerce of the world.[3] It is not known what the Turkish reaction to this note was,[4] but the Russian reply stated categorically that

"The Imperial Cabinet will neither blockade, nor interrupt, nor in any way menace the navigation of the Suez Canal. They consider the Canal as an international work, in which the commerce of the world is interested, and which should be kept free from any attack."[5]

The preceding facts, as well as those mentioned in the previous section regarding tolls and tonnage measurement,[6] very clearly show

[1] *Parl. Pap.*, Commercial No. 14 (1877), C. 1797, p. 33.
[2] *Ibid.*, Commercial No. 19 (1874), C.1075, Annexe 1, p. 331.
[3] *Ibid.*, Russia No. 2 (1877), C.1770, p. 1. See also Egypt No. 1 (1877), C.1766, p. 1.
[4] Badawi in the article mentioned above (p. 48, n. 2) asserts, without again offering any proof, that "Sans procéder à aucun fait de guerre dans le Canal, la Turquie décide cependant que le Canal demeurera ouvert à tout navire neutre et qu'il restera fermé à tout navire ennemi" (p. 15). The present writer is unaware of any diplomatic document or even private writing where reference to this fact is made, though there are many books which assert the opposite.
[5] *Parl. Pap.*, Russia No. 2 (1877), C.1770, p. 3.
[6] See above, pp. 55–56.

how the *de facto* regime of the Suez Canal was all the time being enlarged by new usages. This is not to say that the Sultan had granted new rights to the Powers, except the declaration made at the Constantinople Conference of 1873 with regard to tolls. There is no evidence to show that the Powers considered the new usages as anything but a regime of tolerance.[1] There is, on the other hand, much evidence to support the view that the Powers were very conscious of the regime of internationality as the basis of the legal status of the Canal and that they carefully avoided confusing it with the regime of tolerance.

As late as 1885, the French Government, defending against British objections the Draft Agreement presented to the Paris Conference, remarked that

"...none of the proposed stipulations can be considered as affecting the rights of the Sovereign Power of Egypt, which have been reserved, with the exception of *the servitude to which it has consented from the very commencement for the sake of securing the freedom of the Suez Canal*."[2]

And in the same Conference, the Russian delegate, speaking on the question of fortifications in the canal, expressed himself by saying

"that the Ottoman Sovereign, who has already been so generous in the Concessions granted to the Suez Canal will freely consent to the sacrifices which are indispensable to maintain and to crown with success that great work of universal interest..."[3]

It should not, then, cause surprise to find the Prime Minister of Egypt acknowledging publicly in 1947, before the Security Council, that

"The Suez Canal was an international enterprise from the very beginning, and within a few years after it was opened all the principal Powers of Europe joined with the Ottoman Empire, acting for Egypt, to regulate its traffic, its neutrality and its defence."[4]

After what has been said in the present and previous sections of this chapter concerning both the regime that prevailed in the Canal before 1888 and the intention of the sovereign who established it, it seems impossible to agree with the opinion expressed by the British Prize Court for Egypt in *The Gutenfels* Case,[5] to the effect that "the

---

[1] See the discussions at the Paris Conference of 1885 regarding the word "compléter" especially the remarks by the Austrian and British delegates. *Parl. Pap.*, Egypt No. 19 (1885), C.4599, p. 89.

[2] *Ibid.*, p. 27, Inclosure in No. 52. (Italics mine).

[3] *Ibid.*, p. 111.

[4] U.N. Sec. Council, *Off. Rec.*, 2nd year, No. 70, p. 1756.

[5] *B.C. Prize Cases*, v.1, pp. 108–109.

construction of the Canal had nothing international about it," or
that "there is nothing in these agreements (the Concessions and the
Firman) that can possibly give rights to third parties." Nor is it
possible to accept the view put forward by the Egyptian Foreign
Minister in 1956 before the Security Council that "the system created
by the firman...was a system of tolerance with no binding international obligation on Egypt."[1]

These and similar opinions frequently expressed by writers[2] are
all based on a misconception about the origin of the international
rights granted by the regime of internationality. These writers seem
to think that because the Concessions were acts of internal government they might not give rise to international rights, or, to put
it differently, that to accept international rights derived from the
Concessions would be tantamount to a transmutation of the essentially internal character of those acts into an international instrument.
There is no need of such a transmutation to accept the view propound-
ed throughout this chapter. The 1856 Concession, as well as the
firman and the other agreements, was an act of internal law. Article
14 of that Concession, therefore, was a contract of a private nature
between the Egyptian Government and the Company to maintain
the Canal always open to merchant vessels. But it was also more
than that. By this Article the Viceroy of Egypt, and later on the
Sultan of Turkey, was addressing himself to the nations of the world,
to which he was offering a right of passage through the Canal. This
is shown, as explained in the first section of this chapter, by the care
he took to transmit those instruments to the Powers and by the
negotiations that followed between the Sultan and the principle
Maritime nations regarding the neutrality of the Canal. Once the
offer was tacitly accepted by the Powers, Article 14 without losing
its internal character became the object of an international transaction. The Article had thus given rise to international rights, which
transcended, without transmuting, the essentially private nature of
the acts of Concession. In the future, the territorial sovereign of the
Canal would have, with regard to freedom of navigation, a double
obligation, one of a private nature *vis-à-vis* the Company, and
another of an international character toward the international community.

The system of tolerance, referred to by some writers, might possibly

---

[1] U.N. Sec. Council,*Off. Rec.*, 11th year, 736th meeting, p. 6.
[2] See above, p. 48, n. 2.

concern not the fundamental rights of freedom of navigation definitely established by the regime of internationality, but some of the other usages mentioned above which were accepted in practice by the Sultan of Turkey. It may be convenient for the sake of completeness to inquire whether any of those usages was the result of a new regime accepted by the sovereign, or rather of a mere act of tolerance on his part.

Section III   THE OTHER REGIMES

At the end of Chapter II, a distinction was made, on the one hand, between a regime of internationality and, on the other, the regimes of internationalization, demilitarization and neutralization. The present section is concerned with the latter three.

A regime of internationalization was defined as a regime of international administration. Several attempts to internationalize the Canal were made before 1888. Surprisingly enough the first one was made by de Lesseps himself, who offered to the Powers the Canal for sale in 1871, on account of the financial difficulties in which the Company found itself. The scheme was opposed by both the Viceroy and the Sultan.[1] In December 1875, the Newcastle Chamber of Commerce proposed to the British Government the purchase of the Canal by the countries interested in its trade, with the object of placing it under the control of an International Commission, as had been done with the Danube[2]; and the following year the petition was renewed by the Association of Chambers of Commerce of Great Britain.[3] Both attempts, however, came to nothing.

A different type of internationalization – administration without purchase – was partially achieved by the Ottoman declaration at the Constantinople Conference of 1873, concerning the Canal tolls.[4] This system of consultation and joint decision was later applied to some other questions, such as tonnage measurement[5] or the verification of the ship's papers.[6] However, the purpose of the declaration, which was to secure in a better way freedom of navigation, as well as the

---

[1] *Parl. Pap.*, Egypt No. 2 (1876), C.1392, Appendix.
[2] *Ibid.*, pp. 130–131.
[3] *Ibid.*, Commercial No. 14 (1877), C.1797, p. 27.
[4] See above, p. 55.
[5] See above, p. 56.
[6] *Parl. Pap.*, Commercial No. 12 (1878), C.2010, p. 82, and Commercial No. 23 (1879), C.2399, p. 67.

limited range of its application, would not seem to warrant the conclusion that the Sultan had accepted a regime of international-ization in addition to the one of internationality already granted. It would seem to be more in accord with the facts to qualify the declaration as a supplementary and rather incidental addition to the regime of internationality.

Even less may be said of some other attempts to deal in common with the Canal problems, such as the Constantinople Conference of July 1882 on the occasion of Arabi's rebellion.[1] In this case, far from agreeing to a joint discussion of the matter, the Ottoman Government refused to be represented at the Conference until the 10th meeting, and then, only under strong diplomatic pressure.[2] It may, therefore, be safely concluded that the Sultan of Turkey never agreed to a regime of internationalization in the Canal.

The same conclusion has to be accepted with regard to demil-itarization. Article 4 of the 1854 Concession speaks of "the fortifica-tions which the Government may deem fit to establish," and Article 10 of the Agreement of February 22, 1866, reserves to the Egyptian Government the right to occupy "any position or any strategic point that it considers necessary for the defense of the country."[3] These stipulations are clearly incompatible with a regime of demilitari-zation.

The question of neutralization remains to be considered. Article 14 of the 1856 Concession proclaimed the Canal open forever as a "neutral passage." It has already been suggested[4] that in this Article the Viceroy was envisaging the time of peace as well as that of war; that he was here offering to the world not only a regime of interna-tionality, which concerns solely the time of peace, but also a regime of neutralization, though restricted to merchant vessels, if only the other nations would accept it and be willing to conclude a convention guaranteeing the neutrality of the Canal. For the reasons explained above,[5] this convention never materialized during the period under review, in spite of Lesseps' efforts[6] and the protracted negotiations between the Sultan and the Powers before the *Firman* of March

---

[1] *Ibid.*, Egypt No. 11 (1882), C.3295, p. 6, and Egypt No. 17 (1882), C.3391.
[2] *Ibid.*, Egypt No. 17 (1882), C.3391, p. 203.
[3] See above, p. 50, n. 4 and p. 53, n. 2.
[4] See above, p. 57.
[5] See above, p. 54.
[6] See Lesseps' "Projet de Clauses à Insérer dans le Traité de Paris" and his failure to have it discussed at the Congress of Paris of 1856 in Lesseps, *Lettres.* v. 1, pp. 353 and 362. See also another project of his in *Ibid.*, v. 2, p. 160.

19, 1866.[1] The question of neutralization remained thus in abeyance, pending the final acceptance of the Powers.

At the time of the Franco-German War of 1870 the neutrality of the Canal was *de facto* respected by all.[2] During the Russo-Turkish War of 1877, the Canal remained open even to the warships of the belligerents, and no act of war took place in the Canal or its appproaches, either out of respect for the accepted status of the Canal or out of fear of the British Navy.[2] Lesseps took advantage of the occasion to propose to the British Government a Draft Agreement on Neutralization of the Canal, this time covering even the passage of warships[3]; but the proposal was not considered opportune at the time.

The unsatisfactoriness of the situation did not become evident until Colonel Arabi's rebellion of 1882 forced the British Government to occupy Egypt in order to protect the Canal. Acting upon reports of the plundering of vessels by Arabs in the Canal,[4] British troops were landed at Ismailia on July 31.[5] On August 8 Admiral Hoskins was authorized by the Viceroy to occupy any points of the Isthmus deemed useful for the free traffic on the Canal,[6] and on August 19 all traffic was stopped for twenty-four hours[7]; when it was renewed the next day, British transports had precedence for three days over merchant vessels.[8]

Lesseps protested immediately against, what he called, "the violation of the neutrality of the Suez Canal,"[9] but the British Directors of the Company retorted by pointing out that the French Government had also proposed to land troops and that a German Commandant had actually landed some of his crew at Port Said.[10] This showed in what an unsettled state the whole question of the neutrality of the Canal was.

Realizing the possibilities of conflict that such a situation might entail, Earl Granville proposed to the Powers on January 3, 1883, an agreement "to put upon a clearer footing the position of the Canal

---

[1] See the two notes on neutrality of January 4, 1860, and April 6, 1863, as well as the Vizierial Letter of August 1, 1863, above on pp. 52–53.
[2] See above p. 58.
[3] *Parl. Pap.*, Egypt No. 1 (1877), C.1766, p. 2.
[4] *Ibid.*, Egypt No. 17 (1882), C.3391, p. 140.
[5] *Ibid.*, p. 268.
[6] *Ibid.*, Inclosure in No. 618.
[7] *Ibid.*, Egypt No. 18 (1882), C.3401, p. 6, and Egypt No. 16 (1883), C.3697, p. 7
[8] *Ibid.*, Egypt No. 1 (1883), C.3461, Inclosure in No. 4.
[9] *Ibid.*, Egypt No. 17 (1882), C.3391, p. 268.
[10] *Ibid.*, p. 300.

for the future."[1] Nothing came out of this proposal, but on March 17, 1885, the Powers signed the Declaration of London relative to the Free Navigation of the Suez Canal, in which they "agreed to recognize the urgent necessity for negotiating with the object of sanctioning, by a Conventional Act, the establishment of a definitive regulation guaranteeing at all times, and for all Powers, the freedom of the Suez Canal."[2] As a result of this Declaration an International Commission convened in Paris on March 30, and drew up a Draft Treaty,[3] which with slight modifications became the Constantinople Convention of 1888.

The signing of this Convention became, *a posteriori*, conclusive evidence that the Sultan of Turkey had never accepted before 1888 a regime of neutralization in the Canal. As no treaty of any sort had been concluded before that date – an essential prerequisite in every regime of neutralization – the passing of merchant vessels in war time, as well as of warships in time of peace and of war, which had taken place during that period, must be considered the result of a system of tolerance and mutual understanding rather than of law.[4]

In conclusion, the status of the Suez Canal before 1888 may be described as a practical blending of law and of usage; a legal regime of internationality, guaranteeing freedom of transit for merchant vessels in time of peace, to which certain other practices were added by tolerance of the territorial sovereign. For a number of years the system worked tolerably well, until the crisis of 1882 showed how frail and unsatisfactory it really was. It then became evident that a Convention was needed to "complete" the legal regime already in existence by adding to it a new one – not of tolerance and usage but of law – in order to give to the Canal the "definitive system," as a result of which all vessels of all nations would be assured at all times of free passage through the Canal.[5]

The conclusion drawn from this chapter is also borne out by the discussions of the delegates at the International Commission of Paris in 1885. The Preamble of the French Draft presented to the Commission spoke of

---

[1] *Ibid.*, Egypt No. 2 (1883), C.3462, p. 34, No. 49.
[2] *Ibid.*, Egypt No. 6 (1885), C.4339, p. 9.
[3] *Ibid.*, Egypt No. 19 (1885), C.4599.
[4] Fauchille, *Etude sur le Blocus Maritime*, pp. 186–187; Lawrence, *Essays on Some Disputed Questions in Modern International Law*, p. 42.
[5] See the Preamble to the Constantinople Convention of 1888. Appendix B, below.

"confirming by a Conventional Act the system under which the navigation in the Suez Canal has been placed since its origin by the Concessions...and the Firmans..."[1]

When the paragraph came up for discussion, the Austrian delegate remarked that

"the task of the Sub-Commission not being only to confirm the present system of the Canal, it would be necessary to add after the word "confirm" one of the words "extend" or complete."[2]

On his part, the British delegate thought that

"it would be preferable not to mention the concessions...and the Firmans..., as these Acts only affect merchant-vessels. As they are now occupied in regulating the question of the passage of vessels of war, he proposes to substitute for the words, "the system under which the navigation," in the French preamble, the words, "the definitive system intended"..."[3]

The Preamble, as finally amended and adopted in the Convention of 1888, took account of all the suggestions and incorporated them into the Treaty in the following words

"...[the Powers] being desirous of establishing, by a Conventional Act, a definitive system intended to guarantee, at all times and to all the Powers, the free use of the Suez Maritime Canal, and thus to complete the system under which the navigation of this canal has been placed by the Firman of His Imperial Majesty the Sultan,...sanctioning the Concessions of His Highness the Khedive,..."[4]

It is thus clear, that, in the opinion of the Powers, there had been before 1888 a "system," derived from the Concessions, to regulate navigation in the Canal – what has been termed in this chapter as "regime of internationality" – wich needed to be "completed" in order to establish "a definitive system," that would secure under all circumstances freedom of navigation to all vessels. The Minister of Foreign Affairs of the U. K. very accurately stated in the Security Council that "the Suez Canal Convention of 1888,...constituted the completion rather then the initiation of a system which, taken as a whole, guaranteed passage rights through the Canal. It did not so much originate those rights as confirm them, and place them on a definite international treaty basis."[5] It is time, now, to turn the attention to the new regime established by the Convention of 1888.

[1] *Parl. Pap.*, Egypt No. 19 (1885), C.4599, p. 78, Annex No. 1.
[2] *Ibid.*, p. 89.
[3] *Ibid.*
[4] Appendix B, below.
[5] U.N. Sec. Council, *Off. Rec.*, 11th year, 735th meeting, p. 5.

CHAPTER IV

THE SUEZ CANAL FROM 1888 TO 1956:
THE NEUTRALIZED CANAL

It has been shown in the previous chapter that the Constantinople Convention of 1888 was concluded in order to "complete" the legal regime that had prevailed in the Suez Canal from the beginning of its existence. The purpose of the Convention was to replace the usages that had gradually been introduced in the regime of the Canal by legal rules which would internationally guarantee a definitive and comprehensive system. It will be the object of the next section to describe the most salient features of this system.

Section I THE NEW REGIME

The essence and, at the same time, the aim of the new regime established by the Convention of 1888 is to be found in its first article, which reads:

"The Suez Maritime Canal shall always be free and open, in time of war as in time of peace, to every vessel of commerce or of war, without distinction of flag."[1]

To the regime of internationality, which was characteristic of the Suez Canal in its first period, the Convention now adds freedom of navigation for warships in time of peace, and for merchantships and warships in time of war. It thus brings into being the "definitive system intended to guarantee, at all times and to all Powers, the free use of the Suez Maritime Canal."[2]

This absolute freedom of navigation was so essential a feature of the new Convention that its signatories, not content with laying down the general principle expressed in Article 1, added to it a second paragraph by which they "agree[d] not in any way to interfere with the free use of the Canal, in time of war as in time of peace."[3] And

---

[1] Appendix B, below.
[2] *Ibid.*, Preamble.
[3] *Ibid.*, Art. 1, para. 2.

because Egypt, as the territorial sovereign, and Turkey as the suzerain, may be forced under certain circumstances to take some defensive measures that might conceivably jeopardize the freedom of the
Canal, the Convention takes care to provide that those measures
"shall not interfere with the free use of the Canal,"[1] thereby binding
Turkey and Egypt for the second time to maintain freedom of navigation in the Canal.

However, the obligation incurred by the signatories in the second
paragraph just mentioned does not imply a "guaranty" in the strict
meaning of the term – an undertaking to uphold the Convention and
enforce its provisions – even if use is made of that word in the Preamble to the Convention.[2] What the Preamble intends to convey by the
use of the word "guarantee" is the idea of "securing" the free navigation of the Canal by the acceptance of legal rules, which will supersede
the regime of partial tolerance that prevailed before. In case one of
the signatories violates the Convention by making an attack on the
Canal, no other effect would, it seems, follow than to release the
other signatories from the obligation not to interfere with the free
use of the Canal.[3]

Be that as it may, it was very soon realized by the signatories
that to proclaim the principle of absolute freedom, even if backed
up by a guaranty in the sense just explained, was not enough by
itself to preserve the Canal always open to navigation. The rights of
sovereignty enjoyed by all States, specially during the time of war,
could not easily be reconciled with the principle of freedom unless
some sort of neutralization were agreed upon by all concerned. The
experience of 1882, at the time of Arabi's rebellion, had shown
conclusively that no freedom was possible without neutralization,
nor could neutralization permanently be assured without a treaty.
Such was the origin of the neutrality clauses of the 1888 Convention.
They were intended to secure that absolute freedom, which was the
real aim of the Convention.

Accordingly, Article 4 proclaims as the basic principle that

"no right of war, act of hostility or act having for its purpose to interfere with
the free navigation of the Canal, shall be committed in the Canal and its ports
of access, or within a radius of 3 nautical miles from those ports, even though
the Ottoman Empire should be one of the belligerent Powers."

[1] *Ibid.*, Art. 11.
[2] See the discussion on Art. 1 at the Paris Commission of 1885, *Parl. Pap.*, Egypt
No. 19 (1885), C.4599, p. 90 ff.
[3] *Ibid.*, Egypt No. 1 (1888), C.5255, p. 42.

Warships of belligerents are forbidden to take on fresh supplies in the Canal and its ports of access, except when strictly necessary, to stop while in transit through the Canal, or to stay in the ports of access for more than 24 hours.[1] In time of war, belligerent powers may not discharge or take on troops or war material in the Canal and its ports of access.[2] In addition, the Canal may never be subject to a blockade of any kind.[3]

All these provisions, however, except perhaps the prohibition of blockade,[4] are subject to two exceptions, in so far as they are not meant to stand in the way of the necessary measures for enforcing the execution of the Convention,[5] or the defense of Egypt[6]; even in these two cases, the measures taken cannot interfere with the free use of the Canal.[7]

As a result of the preceding stipulations, the Canal is forever excluded from the region of war, so that no act of war of any kind can legally take place in it, even if Egypt or Turkey is one of the belligerents.[8] The exceptions referred to above can validly be exercised only in the circumstances of space and time in which the execution of the Convention, or the security of Egypt are immediately threatened. The Convention therefore implies "an express and general derogation from the law of war,"[9] for the purpose of securing at all times the free navigation of the Canal.

It is from this viewpoint that the provisions of the Convention should be examined. It will be seen, then, that it does not matter much whether the Canal is described as being "universalized,"[10] or "extraterritorialized,"[11] or "befriedet,"[12] or subject to a "regime of inviolability,"[13] or simply to a "particular regime."[14] The fact is that the Canal has forever been excluded from the region where war can lawfully be prepared or waged. This system has been termed above[15]

---

[1] Art. 4, paras. 2 and 3; see also Art. 7, para. 3.
[2] Art. 5.
[3] Art. 1, para. 3.
[4] Art. 1 is not mentioned either in Art. 9 or 10.
[5] Art. 9.
[6] Art. 10.
[7] Art. 11.
[8] *Parl. Pap.*, Egypt No. 19 (1885), C.4599, p. 43, No. 78.
[9] Visscher, *Les Aspects Juridiques Fondamentaux de la Question de Suez,* (R.G.D.I.P., 3me ser., 29 (1958), 409).
[10] Wilson, *The Suez Canal*, p. 89.
[11] Schonfield, *The Suez Canal in World Affairs*, p. 52.
[12] Dedreux, *Der Suezkanal im internationalen Rechte*, p. 92.
[13] Diena, *Il Canale di Suez ed il Patto de la Società delle Nazioni*, p. 327.
[14] Higgins and Colombos, *The International Law of the Sea*, p. 136, para. 165.
[15] See p. 46, above.

"regime of neutralization." There is thus no reason why the Canal should not be said to be neutralized.[1] The fact that such a neutralization is intended to secure another aim, namely, absolute freedom of navigation in the Canal, does not detract from the essential characteristics of the regime,[2] although, on the other hand, this regime does not adequately describe the whole legal system regulating the Canal.

With the same purpose in mind of better securing the free use of the Canal, the Convention also forbids the keeping of warships in the waters of the Canal, though not in the ports of access,[3] as well as the erection of permanent fortifications on its banks, "the purpose or effect of which might be to interfere with the freedom and complete safety of navigation."[4] The last sentence makes it doubtful whether the Canal can properly be said to be demilitarized,[5] specially in view of the exceptions allowed by Articles 9 and 10. But whether the term "demilitarization" can be used or not to describe the system established by those stipulations, there is little doubt that the purpose of the Convention is to provide for further guarantees to secure freedom of navigation in the Canal.

The same may be said of the rudimentary "regime of internationalization," or international administration, provided for by Articles 8, 9 and 10. The Agents in Egypt of the Signatory Powers are charged to watch over the execution of the Convention and to inform the Egyptian Government of any danger that may threaten the security and free passage of the Canal.[6] In addition, the Signatory Powers of the Declaration of London of 1885[7] are to be given notice[8] of any measures that the Viceroy of Egypt or the Sultan of Turkey may take in accordance with the provisions of Articles 9 and 10.

The Convention of 1888 may thus be seen in perspective as a complete legal system by which a new regime of absolute freedom of

---

[1] Caution should be exercised not to confuse this type of neutralization with neutralization of States. See Oppenheim-Lauterpacht, *International Law*, v. 1 (8th ed.), p. 243.

[2] Cammand, *op. cit.*, p. 183; Hains, *Neutralization of the Panama Canal*, (A.J.I.L., 3 (1909) 363); Fauchille, *Traité de Droit International Public*, t. 1, 2me partie, p. 331; Aglietti, *Il Canale di Suez ed i Rapporti Anglo-Egiziani*, pp. 48–49; Contuzzi, *La Neutralizzazione del Canale di Suez e la Diplomazia Europea*, p. 41; Avram, *op. cit.*, p. 50.

[3] Art. 7, paras. 1 and 2.

[4] Art. 8, para. 3 and Art. 11.

[5] See above, p. 46.

[6] Art. 8, paras. 1 and 2.

[7] All the signatories to the 1888 Convention except Spain and The Netherlands.

[8] Art 9, para. 2 and Art. 10, para. 2.

navigation in the Canal – going far beyond the previous "regime of internationality" – is permanently[1] established, the preservation of which is assured by a legal guaranty given by all the signatories, and a provision for a "regime of neutralization" supplemented by both a system approaching "demilitarization" and a rather imperfect "regime of internationalization."

Section II   LEGAL EFFECTS OF THE CONVENTION

Article 17 of the Constantinople Convention provided for the exchange of ratifications "within a month or sooner if possible." It may, however, very well be doubted whether the Convention entered into force as soon as the ratifications were exchanged. The reservation made by the British delegates at the Suez Canal Commission of 1885, to the effect that England would retain her freedom of action so long as she was in occupation of Egypt,[2] had been renewed by Lord Salisbury and communicated to the Powers in 1887.[3] According to the interpretation given at the time by France and approved by the British Minister, the effect of the reservation was to suspend the application of those provisions only that were incompatible with the actual situation in Egypt.[4] Lord Curzon, however, speaking to the House of Commons in 1898 stated expressly that "the Convention... is certainly in existence, but...has not been brought into practical operation."[5] And the Anglo-French Agreement of 1904 would seem to confirm this last interpretation, for Article 6 proclaimed that "His Britannic Majesty's Government declare that they adhere to the stipulations of the treaty of the 29th October, 1888, and that they agree to their being put in force."[6]

On the other hand, the attitude of the Powers and specially of Great Britain during the Spanish-American War tends rather to suggest that the validity of the Convention and its application both in time of peace and in time of war was accepted by all.[7] It was precisely because the Convention was considered binding that Great

---

[1] Art. 14.
[2] Parl. Pap., Egypt No. 1 (1888), C.5255, p. 36.
[3] 61 Parl. Deb. (4th ser.) 667 (1898).
[4] Doc. Dipl., Négociations relatives au Règlement International pour le libre usage du Canal de Suez 1886–1887, pp. 114–5.
[5] 61 Parl. Deb. (4th ser.) 667 (1898).
[6] Parl. Pap., France No. 1 (1904), Cd. 1952, Inclosure 1.
[7] U.S. For. Rel. (1898), p. 982, No. 438 and p. 983.

Britain was able to interpret some of its provisions in a manner prejudicial to the best interests of Spain.[1] The same attitude was adopted by the Powers during the Russo-Japanese War of 1904, when rules regarding coaling by belligerents were enacted on February 10, in accordance with the provisions of the Convention.[2]

Be that as it may, the Anglo-French Agreement of April 8, 1904 followed, as it was, by similar agreements with other powers,[3] ended all uncertainty, for Great Britain formally agreed to the 1888 Convention being put in force.[4] At the same time, it was resolved among the Powers that some of the stipulations contained in Article 8 of that Convention, concerning the very imperfect "regime of internationalization," should remain in abeyance.[5] Thus, the same Agreement that brought legally into operation the Constantinople Convention of 1888, was also instrumental in bringing about its partial alteration.

After the Agreement of 1904, if not before, the Constantinople Convention began to produce all its legal effects. From the viewpoint of the Ottoman Empire the effect of the Convention was to impose on Egypt and Turkey the obligation to maintain the Canal always free and open to navigation. This obligation was intended to be perpetual,[6] as was also incidentally remarked by the Permanent Court in *The Wimbledon* Case,[7] and consequently, in accord with the considerations made above,[8] it should be qualified as an obligation of a real nature, permanently attached to the territory.[9]

On the other hand, the Convention gives Turkey and Egypt a right *erga omnes* to demand from any belligerent that the Canal be excluded forever from the region of any war.[10] As a result, the Canal remains permanently neutralized, in so far as no act of war can legally be committed in the Canal and its approaches under any circumstances, even if Turkey or Egypt is one of the belligerents, and consequently, the use of the Canal "whether by belligerent men-of-war, or by

[1] See Cammand, *op. cit.*, pp. 217–219 and Crabitès, *The Spoliation of Suez*, pp. 232–234.

[2] *B.F.St. Pap.*, 102 (1908–1909) 591.

[3] See above p. 12.

[4] *Parl. Pap.*, France No. 1 (1904), Cd. 1952, Inclosure 1: Art. 6.

[5] *Ibid.*, Art. 6.

[6] Constantinople Convention, Art. 14.

[7] P.C.I.J., *Ser. A*, No. 1 (1923), p. 25.

[8] See above pp. 42–43.

[9] Cammand, *op. cit.*, pp. 193–194; Charles–Roux, *op. cit.*, v. 2, p. 111; Diena, *Il Canale di Suez ed il Patto de la Società delle Nazioni*, p. 333.

[10] *Doc. Dipl.*, Négociations relatives au Règlement International pour le libre usage du Canal de Suez 1886–1887, p. 107.

belligerent or neutral merchant ships carrying contraband, is not regarded as incompatible with the neutrality of the riparian sovereign."[1]

From the viewpoint of the international community the effect of the 1888 Convention is, first and foremost, to grant a right to every nation of the world to navigate the Canal freely under any circumstances, either in time of peace or in time of war, even if Turkey or Egypt is one of the belligerents.[2] At the same time each nation is burdened with the obligation to respect the neutrality of the Canal, and consequently to refrain from committing any war-like acts in the Canal and its approaches, even in the case of a war being waged against the Ottoman Empire.

Such a broad obligation imposed on each and all nations of the world seems to have been taken for granted by almost everyone from the very beginning. Already at the Paris Commission of 1885, the Dutch Delegate had proposed to consider every violation of the free navigation of the Canal "as an offence against international law."[3] Although the proposal was not formally adopted, its substance seems to have been commonly accepted in the language of the law, though not, perhaps, so often in the practice of states.[4] The rationale of the majority opinion in *The Wimbledon* case[5] and the express statements of the minority Judges[6] clearly show that all of them took for granted the obligation imposed on all nations to respect the neutrality of the Suez Canal. The same may be said of practically all writers of international law, though here emphasis is often laid on freedom of navigation rather than on the related aspect of neutralization; even among those who treat of the latter question, there is seldom found in their writings more than a perfunctory mention of the source of the obligation.[7] And yet, this is the *crux* of the matter, for how can the fact of the obligation be accepted unless it be possible to justify legally the imposition of such an obligation?

The problem, therefore, confronting the international community is not so much to find out the specific provisions of the Convention and to assert their obligation as to know how those provisions become

---

[1] P.C.I.J., *Ser. A*, No. 1 (1923), *Wimbledon* Case, p. 25.

[2] Arts. 1 and 11.

[3] *Parl. Pap.*, Egypt No. 19 (1885), C.4599, p. 202.

[4] See below Section III of this chapter.

[5] *Ser. A*, No. 1 (1923), pp. 25 and 28.

[6] *Ibid.*, pp. 39, 43 and 46.

[7] See for instance Poiaga, *Suez: Aspetti del Problema*, pp. 82–83 and Avram, *op. cit.*, pp. 47, 48 and 55.

binding on the international community. It is on this aspect of the problem that the whole question of the legal effects of the Constantinople Convention hinges.

The 1888 Convention was signed at Constantinople on October 29 by Great Britain, Germany, Austria-Hungary, Spain, France, Italy, The Netherlands, Russia and Turkey. For all these States, therefore, the Convention began to produce the aforesaid legal effects as soon as it entered into force.[1] As a result, the nine Powers, who already enjoyed the right of sending through the Canal their merchant ships in time of peace under the previous "regime of internationality," acquired now in addition the much wider rights of absolute freedom of navigation; at the same time, they became bound by the obligations derived from the "regime of neutralization."[2]

The same legal position was to be enjoyed by any other acceding State. According to Article 16, all States were to be invited to accede to the Convention, but in fact none seems to have done it.[3] Thus, with the exception of the original Signatory Powers, all the countries of the world are, regarding the 1888 Convention, in the category of non-signatory States. With regard to them therefore the question of the obligatory character of the Convention remains still open.

There is, however, among the non-signatories a small group of States, which might be entitled to special consideration. This is the group of the so-called successor States, that is, States which at the time of the Constantinople Convention, or thereafter, were parts of the territory of some Signatory Power, or subject at least to its suzerainty. Chief among them, because of her obvious connexion with the problem at hand, is Egypt.

It has been suggested above[4] that the regime of internationality, which was established in the Canal by the Viceroy of Egypt and confirmed later on by the Sultan of Turkey, creates obligations of a real nature, permanently attached to the territory. By virtue of Article 14 of the Second Concession of 1856, Egypt is perpetually bound to allow in time of peace free navigation in the Canal to merchant ships.

The 1888 Convention, of which Egypt was not a signatory, created also obligations of a real nature, in so far as they were accepted by

---

[1] See above pp. 70–71.
[2] The signatories of the Declaration of London assumed, in addition, special rights and obligations. See Art. 9, para. 2 and Art. 10, para. 2.
[3] Whittuck, *International Canals*, p. 22.
[4] See above p. 42.

Turkey, the suzerain of Egypt, and referred to the establishment of a permanent regime over a part of the Turkish Empire, to which territory they became attached independently of the changes that might later on affect its sovereignty. In addition, the Convention imposed specific obligations on, and granted special rights to Egypt, as the country most immediately connected with the Canal.[1] It may then be said that Egypt, though not a signatory of the Convention, was bound from the beginning by many of its provisions. When at last her independence was proclaimed in 1922, Egypt found herself not only the sole legal master of the Canal but also bound forever by all the obligations contracted by the former Ottoman Empire with regard to the Canal. She, thus, necessarily became a party to the Constantinople Convention on the double ground of being a successor to Turkey specially connected with that Convention, and at the same time, the sovereign of the territory over which the Canal ran.

This situation was expressly recognized by Egypt in 1938. On April 16, Great Britain and Italy signed in Rome a *Declaration regarding the Suez Canal*, whereby they reaffirmed "their intention always to respect and abide by the provisions of the Convention... [of Constantinople], which guarantees at all times and for all Powers the free use of the Suez Canal."[2] The same day, the Egyptian Ambassador to Italy informed both Governments, through an exchange of Notes, that "the Egyptian Government, as the territorial Power concerned, take note of the intention of the Italian Government and the Government of the U. K. and associate themselves therewith."[3]

The same position was taken by Egypt in 1947, when the Egyptian Prime Minister proclaimed in the Security Council that "the Canal is an international artery open to all nations in time of peace and in time of war."[4] Lastly, in the Anglo-Egyptian Agreement of October 19, 1954, the two contracting Governments "express[ed] the determination to uphold the Convention guaranteeing the freedom of navigation of the Canal signed at Constantinople on the 29th of October, 1888."[5]

It is thus clear that Egypt is not only bound by the provisions of the Constantinople Convention, as the successor to Turkey and the State over whose territory the Canal flows, but has also repeatedly

---

[1] Arts. 8, 9, 10 and 14.
[2] *L.N.T.S.*, 195 (1939) 88: Annex 8.
[3] *Ibid.*, p. 108.
[4] U.N. Sec. Council, *Off. Rec.*, 2nd year, No. 70, p. 1755.
[5] *U.N.T.S.*, 210 (1955) 26: Art. 8. For the Declaration of Egypt of April 24, 1957, see below pp. 108–110 and Appendix D.

recognized the obligations emanating from that Convention. Fears expressed on that account by some writers,[1] should be considered absolutely groundless.

Egypt then stands in a special category of its own among the successor States. There are two other States whose legal position regarding the Constantinople Convention has also been clarified. By Articles 234 (10) of the Treaty of St. Germain and 217 (10) of that of Trianon[2] respectively, Austria and Hungary, as the successors to the former Austro-Hungarian Empire, have accepted to be bound by the provisions of the Constantinople Convention of 1888, and stand therefore with regard to them in the same position as that formerly enjoyed by the Austro-Hungarian Empire, or for that matter, by any of the original Signatory Powers.

As for the rest of the successor States, the situation is far from clear. The Egyptian and Soviet representatives in the Security Council argued in 1954 in favor of enlarging the circle of the signatories of the Convention to include their Successors.[3] The proposal, though not followed up by any other State, was not rejected either. But, what is a successor State? Presumably under that name such States as Poland and Czechoslovakia would be included as successors to the Austro-Hungarian Empire. Would Finland also be included as successor to the Russian Empire? What about the Dominions of the British Commonwealth that have long since become sovereign and independent States? Should the concept of successor State be extended to include former Mandates and Colonies? These are but a few of the questions that might be raised in connexion with the problem of successor States.

In view of the difficulty of arriving at a satisfactory answer to the foregoing questions, all successor States, with the triple exception of Egypt, Austria and Hungary already mentioned, will be considered for the purpose of the present study as simply non-signatory States. It is with regard to them that the question of the obligatory character of the 1888 Convention must now be solved.

The question thus posed is but an application of the wider problem, already dealt with above,[4] of International Conventions and Third States. According to the conclusions reached there a non-signatory

---

[1] See for instance Watt, *Britain and the Suez Canal*, p. 3.

[2] Martens, *N.R.G.*, 3me ser., v. 11, p. 691 and v. 12, p. 423.

[3] U.N. Sec. Council, *Off. Rec.*, 9th year, 662nd meeting, para. 47 and 664th meeting, para. 53.

[4] See above pp. 30–32.

State may be bound by the stipulations of an international treaty in any of the following three ways: tacit acceptance, international settlement and custom.

Some writers have expressed the opinion that the provisions of the Constantinople Convention are binding on non-signatory States through their tacit acceptance, as manifested in the use of the Canal.[1] According to their reasoning, whoever uses the Canal accepts, by that very fact, all the conditions attached to it, among which the provisions on neutralization are paramount. Therefore, so the conclusion goes, by the mere use of the Canal non-signatory States become bound by all the stipulations of the Convention.

The reasoning, though lucid and simple, is hardly applicable to the 1888 Convention. First of all, it is very doubtful, as pointed out before,[2] whether a treaty with an accession clause can be accepted tacitly. Secondly, if it is argued that in chapter II the theory of appropriation of rights has been accepted as sufficient for the purpose of establishing an international canal by treaty[3] and that perhaps the same should also prove sufficient here, the reply must be in the negative. The 1888 Convention not only grants rights, which can be appropriated, but also imposes very heavy obligations indissolubly united to those rights, which effectively restrict the freedom of action of the participant State whose acceptance, therefore, by such a State can never be taken for granted. Thirdly, if it is further argued that as the State using the Canal implicitly accepts the ordinary conditions attached to that use (paying tolls, complying with the rules of navigation, etc.) so it must also accept the obligations regarding neutralization imposed by the Convention, the answer is that there is no parity between the two types of obligations. It might, perhaps, be admitted that there is a broad similarity between the obligation of paying tolls and of not damaging the Canal while in transit, but there is absolutely no connexion between the former obligation and the obligation of not blockading or attacking the Canal in a future war between that State and Egypt, as it is required by the Convention. Lastly, even if this opinion were accepted, it would only explain the obligatory character of the Convention with regard to the users of the Canal. The convention would not bind the non-users.

A second way of imposing the obligations of a treaty on non-sig-

---

[1] Poiaga, *op. cit.*, pp. 82–83 and Avram, *op. cit.*, pp. 47, 48 and 75.
[2] See above pp. 31–32.
[3] *Ibid.*

natory States is through an international settlement. There is little doubt that the Great Powers in 1888 believed, in a general way, the Constantinople Convention to be such a settlement – an opinion which was probably shared by more than one State. When some of the lesser European Powers were refused admission to the Paris Commission of 1885, the refusal was justified by the French Foreign Minister on the following grounds:

"...j'estime, quant à moi, que le fait de les admettre à participer à des délibéra-tions portant sur des questions de politique générale réservées jusqu'ici aux Grandes Puissances risquerait de constituer un précedent que celles-ci pour-raient regretter dans l'avenir."[1]

There are some writers, even today, who consider the 1888 Conven-tion to be a law-making treaty, or an international settlement,[2] though, perhaps, there are many more who reject that view.[3] The difficulty with the opinion expressed by the former group lies in the fact that the Convention has established a regime of neutralization of the Canal which directly affects many rights of the States, and that to have such broad obligations imposed by a small group of States on the great majority of the international community without their consent seems to go beyond the powers of any group, however powerful and influential their members might be.

The case is different when the question is one of neutralizing a State. Assuming that such a neutralization is an international set-tlement – an assumption with which not all States would agree – still the obligation imposed on non-signatories not to attack the neu-tralized State, in any case, is balanced by the security it brings to the non-signatory Powers of never being attacked by it. However, in the case of the Constantinople Convention there is no such com-parable consideration being offered for the broad limitations that would be imposed on the non-signatory States. While, in case of war, Egypt would be freed from the fear of an attack on the Canal, she, in turn, would not be restricted from attacking the other bellig-erent on any part of its territory.

The doctrine of international settlements is still in too vague and ill-defined a state to allow us, in a particular case and in the absence of a decision handed down by an international Court, to draw any definite conclusions from a mere examination of its general principles.

[1] *Parl. Pap.*, Egypt No. 19 (1885), C.4599, Inclosure in N. 57.
[2] See for instance Avram, *op. cit.*, p. 150.
[3] See Dedreux, *Der Suezkanal im internationalen Rechte*, p. 81 and writers mentioned in footnote.

The practice of States with regard to the Constantinople Convention then remains as the only sure test of the obligatory character of that Convention. And this brings us to an examination of the third way of imposing obligations on non-signatory States; namely, custom, of which the practice of States is an essential element.

To be sure, an inquiry into the practice of States with regard to an international settlement is not identical with one on the practice of States with regard to custom. The former is concerned in ascertaining whether the States of the world have acted, from the beginning of the international settlement, under the impression that they were bound by its provisions; whereas the purpose of the latter is to inquire whether at the present time the States act on the belief that they are bound by the provisions of the Convention, though no such rule existed at the time the Convention entered into force.

However, both inquiries, though not identical, display sufficient points of similarity among themselves to have them most conveniently carried out jointly. The third section of this chapter is devoted to both of these inquiries.

Section III   THE CONVENTION IN THE PRACTICE OF STATES

The first test of the attitude of non-signatory States toward the Constantinople Convention was provided by the Spanish-American War of 1898. Upon the outbreak of hostilities the American Ambassador in London sounded the British Government as to their attitude with regard to American warships using the Canal. The Ambassador reported back the results of his interview with the British Foreign Minister in the following words:

> "I gathered from his remarks that he had no idea that any power would make any protest against our use of the Canal, nor that any protest would hold if it were made. The attitude of the British Government is that we are unquestionably entitled to the use of the canal for war ships."[1]

It is hard to believe that the American Government would have made such an inquiry if they had been under the impression of being bound by the Convention, or that the British Minister would have given such an answer had he been convinced of the binding character of that international settlement upon all the nations of the world. It is probably true to say that both Governments believed in a vague

---

[1] *U.S. For. Rel.* (1898), p. 982, No. 438.

and general way that there was a right to navigate the Canal, enjoyed by all the nations without, however, giving much thought to the consequences that right might entail with regard to the other provisions of the Convention.

This conclusion seems also to be borne out by the reply given by the Department of State to the foregoing communication, where the object of the American inquiry was described thus:

"1. It was desired to avoid even the possibility of objection being made to the use of the canal by our ships of war...

"2. The Department, while recognizing the general and unrestricted purpose of the convention...was not disposed wholly to rely upon it or formally to appeal to it, since the United States is not one of the signatory powers."[1]

In the opinion of the American Government then, non-signatory powers were believed to be in quite a different position from the signatories, and their rights and obligations, in a rather vague and ill-defined state. Such an opinion is not compatible with a belief in the binding character of the Convention as an international settlement.

The second test came with the Russo-Japanese War of 1904. On February 10 the Egyptian Government enacted some *Rules regarding Coaling by Belligerent Warships in the Suez Canal*, which were based on the provisions of the 1888 Convention and equally applied to both belligerents, though Japan was not one of the signatories.[2] On the whole, the Convention seems to have been kept by the belligerents, but there is nothing on record to show what Japan's attitude was toward the Convention.

On the other hand, the Italo-Turkish War of 1911-1912, though fought between two signatories of the Convention, is interesting because the Egyptian Government for the first time made use of the powers granted by Article 9 to enforce the execution of the Convention, and this against the territorial sovereign himself. Five Turkish gunboats, which failed to leave Port-Said after 24 hours, as required by Article 4, were boarded and disarmed by the Egyptian authorities, without any protest being made by Turkey.[3]

Summing up the practice of States with regard to the Constantinople Convention before the First World War, it may be said that the

---

[1] *Ibid.*, p. 983, No. 746.

[2] *B.F.St. Pap.*, 102 (1908–1909) 591.

[3] Rapisardi–Mirabelli, *La Guerre Italo-Turque et le Droit des Gens*, (R.D.I.L.C., 2me ser., 15 (1913) 115); Hoskins, *The Suez Canal in Time of War*, (*Foreign Affairs*, 14 (1935–36) 98).

Convention was kept by all the Powers concerned in time of peace as well as in time of war, but there is no evidence to show that the non-signatory States had accepted that Convention as an international settlement and consequently, that they acted under the conviction of being bound by its provisions. If, generally speaking, they believed in their right to navigate the Canal, the belief was ill-founded in so far as it was wholly divorced from the other provisions of the Convention, specially those on neutralization, and must rather be considered the result of a usage of long standing, confirmed in their minds later on by Article 1 of the 1888 Convention.

On the other hand, it might be argued with good reason that, since signatories and non-signatories alike had abided by the provisions of the Convention both in time of peace and in time of war up to the beginning of the First World War, a customary rule of international law was growing up in 1914, whereby the stipulations of the Constantinople Convention would in time become binding on the international community.

The First World War affected in many ways the Constantinople Convention. On August 5, 1914, the Egyptian Government issued a Proclamation according to which the Canal was to be open to the merchant vessels of all nations.[1] As for warships, the Proclamation only provided that British warships would act "suivant la Convention du Canal de Suez de 1888,"[2] but in fact the Canal was closed from the outbreak of hostilities to vessels of war of the Central Powers, as a measure of protection for the Canal.[3]

The same reason was given for the general precautionary order, issued by the General officer Commanding British troops, that no enemy vessel was to enter the Canal,[4] and the British Prize Court for Egypt stated in the *Gutenfels* case that

"...the Convention has to be interpreted with a view to the altered circumstances which have arisen...generally speaking, at all times, whether nations are at war or peace, there is a right of free passage (that is, entrance, passage through, and exit – nothing more) for ships of all nations through the Canal; but under certain circumstances, such as danger to the free navigation of the Canal, I consider that this privilege might be curtailed."[5]

On the same grounds of protecting the Canal, vessels were searched within the three-mile limit, at least since March 1915, their cargoes

[1] *B.F.St. Pap.*, 109 (1915) 431–433.
[2] *Ibid.*, Art. 20 (d).
[3] Whittuck, *op. cit.*, p. 23.
[4] See *B.C. Prize Cases: The Concadoro*, v. 2, pp. 65–66.
[5] *Ibid.*, v. 1, p. 118.

examined and the information thus gained, as to war contraband or enemy's cargo, passed on to ships outside the territorial belt with a view to formal capture there.[1]

The protection of Egypt and of the Canal was also invoked by the British Government as justification for the powerful fortifications that were erected on both banks of the Canal, though this fact was in turn adduced by Turkey in her Circular Letter of May 1918 to all the Neutral Powers, as justifying her attack on the Canal in the previous January and subsequent aerial attacks.[2]

There is little doubt that the Convention was clearly violated in its letter and its spirit, specially Articles 1, 4 and 11, by the measures just mentioned. The interpretation given by the British Prize Court resulted in a *de facto* closure of the Canal to enemy vessels. To assert that for the purpose of protecting the Canal in order that it may always be open to the vessels of all nations, it was necessary to close it to one's own enemies, might be admired as a Machiavellian intent to rationalize one's acts, but does not carry much conviction.

Perhaps the same could not be said of the British Notification of October 23, 1914, whereby all enemy ships which had taken refuge at the outbreak of hostilities in the Suez Canal were taken outside the three-mile limit and there captured as prizes by the British navy.[3] It may be argued in justification of this measure that the Canal might otherwise have been entirely blocked, although the ways in which it was carried out at times – such as previously disabling their engines or destroying their wireless sets[4] – might be considered as an act of war, contrary to Article 4 of the Convention.

The British Prize Court for Egypt, in a series of decisions handed down during the war, not only defended the measure itself but even attempted to justify the acts of war committed in carrying it out as having taken place outside the limits where the Convention was applicable: "The object of the Convention is to ensure a free passage through the Canal, and nothing else, and all prohibitions against acts of hostility within the Canal precincts are framed with that object

---

[1] Whittuck, *op. cit.*, pp. 81–84; Berkol, *Le Statut Juridique actuel des Portes Maritimes Orientales de la Méditerranée*, p. 393.

[2] U.N. Sec. Council, *Off. Rec.*, 6th year, 555th meeting, p. 8; Molfino, *Il Canale di Suez e il suo regime internazionale,*p. 93; Schonfield, *The Suez Canal in World Affairs*, pp. 71–72.

[3] *B.F.St. Pap.*, 108 (1914²) 154; *B.C. Prize Cases*, v. 3, pp. 503–504.

[4] *B.C. Prize Cases: The Marquis Becquehem*, v. 2, p. 62; Crabitès, *The Spoliation of Suez*, p. 240.

and that alone."[1] It follows that, if the Convention was not applicable, the Canal and its ports of access reverted, in all respects, to their original position as parts of Egypt, and consequently, were to be considered "enemy territory" as far as the Central Powers were concerned, since Great Britain was in occupation of Egypt.[2] It is difficult, however, to reconcile this conclusion with the provisions on neutralization of the Convention.

Be that as it may, there were enough indisputable violations of the Convention during the First World War, as mentioned above, to justify the protests made by the Central Powers.[3] The British Government was careful to keep the letter of the Convention, if not the spirit, whenever feasible, and the rest of the countries of the world were either readily convinced by the British excuses or sufficiently prudent not to raise their voices. The net result would seem to have been an almost universal acquiescence in the measures taken, however those measures might have been in contradiction to the Constantinople Convention.

The Convention was also considerably affected in practice by the peculiar and ill-defined relationship between Great Britain and Egypt. Before 1914, that relationship seems to have been nothing else than a British military occupation of Egypt, though, as a result of it, several provisions of the Constantinople Convention were modified.[4] On December 18, 1914, a British Protectorate over Egypt was proclaimed,[5] which was later recognized in the Treaties of Peace by the Central Powers.[6] In the same Treaties, the enemy States agreed also to transfer to the British Government the powers conferred on the Sultan by the 1888 Convention,[7] though this transfer was legally impossible, in so far as Great Britain did not stand in relation to Egypt in the same position as the former Ottoman Empire, and contrary to the principle of equality as proclaimed in Article 12 of the Convention. But no protest seems to have been raised against this new alteration of the Constantinople Convention.

On February 28, 1922, the Protectorate over Egypt was terminated,

---

[1] *B.C. Prize Cases: The Gutenfels*, v. 1, p. 111, confirmed later by the Privy Council, *Ibid.*, v. 2, p. 43. See also *The Pindos, Ibid.*, v. 2, p. 149.

[2] *Ibid.: The Gutenfels*, v. 2, pp. 40–41; *The Derflinger*, v. 2, p. 44; *The Marquis Becquehem*, v. 2, p. 59; *The Concadoro*, v. 2, p. 65.

[3] See above, p. 81, n. 2.

[4] See above p. 70.

[5] *B.F.St. Pap.*, 108 (1914²) 185.

[6] See above, p. 13, n. 7.

[7] T. of Versailles, art. 152; T. of St. Germain, art. 107; T. of Trianon, art. 91; T. of Lausanne, arts. 16, 17, 19.

and Egypt declared an independent sovereign State.[1] Among the
matters, however, absolutely reserved to the discretion of the British
Government, for the time being, were "the security of the communications of the British Empire in Egypt" and "the defence of Egypt."
These two points were not disposed of until the Treaty of August
26, 1936, between Great Britain and Egypt, by which

> "His Majesty the King of Egypt, until such time as the high contracting
> parties agree that the Egyptian army is in a position to ensure by its own
> resources the liberty and entire security of navigation of the Canal, authorizes
> His Majesty the King and Emperor to station forces in Egyptian territory
> in the vicinity of the Canal...with a view to ensuring in co-operation with the
> Egyptian forces the defence of the Canal."[2]

It is too evident that the foregoing stipulation runs contrary not
only to Article 12 of the Convention, already referred to, but even to
the very essence of Articles 9 and 10, since, if Egypt had become a
truly sovereign and independent State, as proclaimed in Articles 1
and 3 of the 1936 Treaty, there was no legal basis whatever in the
1888 Convention, even with Egypt's consent, for the stationing of
British troops in the vicinity of the Canal.[3] Once Egypt had become
independent, all the Signatory Powers of the Declaration of London
of March 17, 1885, stood in exactly the same position in relation to
Egypt, and no privilege could be granted to any one of them without
altering in an essential way the provisions of Articles 9 and 10 of the
Convention. But, again, no official protest seems to have been voiced
at the time.

The only effect of the privilege thus granted to Great Britain was
to subject in the future the Canal to the vicissitudes of British foreign
policy, as was made abundantly clear in the Second World War.

Upon the outbreak of hostilities, on September 3, 1939, the
Egyptian Government yielding to British pressure enacted a Military Proclamation providing for the inspection of ships at Port-
Said and at Suez,[4] though Egypt remained neutral, almost until the
end of the war. The Canal was from the beginning closed to hostile
shipping,[5] and, as the war proceeded, it became increasingly reserved
to warships and military transports of the united nations so that even

[1] *Egypt No. 1* (1922), Cmd. 1592, p. 29.
[2] *L.N.T.S.*, 173 (1936–1937) 406: Art. 8.
[3] Sottile, *Méditerranée, Suez et Liberté de navigation*,(*R.D.I.S.D.P.*, 18 (1940) 127);
Ambrosini, *La Situazione Internazionale dell'Egitto e il Regime del Canale di Suez*,
pp. 34–35.
[4] Egypt, *Journal Officiel*, 4 Septembre 1939, Proclamation No. 4.
[5] Watt, *Britain and the Suez Canal*, p. 2.

neutral commercial vessels were not allowed to pass through it at times.[1] British warships used to revictual and take in stores in the Canal and its ports of access, embark and disembark troops and war materiel there, and even be stationed in the waters of the Canal,[2] against the explicit provisions of Articles 4, 5 and 7.

In view of such flagrant violations of the Constantinople Convention, it is not surprising that German and Italian aircraft repeatedly bombed the Canal and made efforts to destroy it or, at least, to put it out of order for the rest of the war.[3] Nor, under similar circumstances, was such an intention attributable only to Axis unscrupulosity. On June 30, 1942, President Roosevelt and Harry L. Hopkins drafted the following telegram, which was subsequently dispatched to General Marshall:

"On the assumption that the Delta will be evacuated within ten days and the Canal blocked, I ask the following question: What assurances have we that the Canal will be really blocked? Do we know the specific plan?...An effective blocking of the Canal is essential."

Marshall replied that the British Navy could block the Suez Canal so effectively that it was estimated that six months would be required to reopen it.[4]

The conclusion, then, would seem to be that during the Second World War the Constantinople Convention became for the belligerents a piece of paper to be put aside whenever military considerations demanded it. Not even a pretense was made, as had been done in the First World War, to keep the letter of the Convention. As for the neutral Powers, they were either too weak or too disinterested to raise any objections.[5]

The background of the two World Wars has to be kept in mind in order to understand the increasingly important role which Egypt began to play in relation to the Suez Canal. On May 28, 1947, an Egyptian Note addressed to the Diplomatic Missions in Cairo, required all warships wishing to pass through the Canal to notify the Egyptian Authorities ten days in advance.[6] Although such an order was in clear contravention to Article 1 of the Constantinople Convention, no Power protested.

---

[1] el–Hefnaoui, *Les Problèmes Contemporains posés par le Canal de Suez*, p. 185.
[2] U.N. Sec. Council, *Off. Rec.*, 6th year, 555th meeting, p. 8.
[3] Rammontel, *Le Canal de Suez, grande oeuvre française,*pp. 151–152.
[4] Sherwood, *Roosevelt and Hopkins. An Intimate History*, p. 595.
[5] U.N. Sec. Council,*Off. Rec.*, 6th year, 549th meeting, p. 19; Avram, *op. cit.*, p. 94.
[6] Cited in Avram, *op. cit.*, p. 104.

On May 15, 1948, the Palestinian War broke out, and, as a result of it, the Egyptian Government introduced a series of measures which profoundly affected the regime of the Canal. By a Proclamation of the same day a service of inspection was established at Suez and Port-Said for all ships passing through the Canal.[1] The inspecting officer was to confiscate munitions and goods of all sorts going to or coming from Israel, as war-contraband.[2] Israeli vessels of commerce and of war were to be immediately confiscated, without any need of having them submitted to the Prize Council.[3] Even after the Egyptian-Israeli Armistice of February 1949, most of the measures described were maintained in one form or another,[4] on the ground that an armistice does not put an end to the war but merely suspends military operations.

The fact that the aforesaid measures impaired the freedom of navigation in the Canal contrary to the provisions of Articles 1 and 11 of the Constantinople Convention, and that some of them constituted acts of war forbidden by Articles 4 and 7 is not open to discussion. The Egyptian Prize Court of Alexandria, however, has maintained that "the prohibitions contained in those articles cannot interfere with the natural right of a State to preserve its own existence," and consequently that "the provisions of Article 11 of the Convention...cannot be construed as a restriction upon the rights of Egypt," its only purpose being "to confirm what is said in Article 1 about free passage through the Canal in time of war and peace; but reasonable and necessary measures taken by Egypt do not interfere with such passage."[5]

This is in essence the position taken by the Egyptian Government and repeated again and again by its representatives in the Security Council.[6] There is no doubt that Egypt is a sovereign and independent State, but her freedom of action, as that of every other State, is limited by the international engagements to which she is a party. If she is bound by the provisions of the Constantinople Convention, then her sovereign rights over the Canal are permanently restricted,

---

[1] Egypt, *Journal Officiel*, 15 Mai 1948, Proclam. No. 5.

[2] *Ibid.*, 19 Mai 1948, Procl. No. 13; 6 Juin 1948, Avis du Gouverneur Militaire Général; 28 Juin 1948, Avis.

[3] *Ibid.*, 8 Juillet 1948, Procl. No. 38, Art. 24.

[4] *Ibid.*, 5 Juin 1950, Loi No. 50; 26 Juin 1950, Loi No.32; U.N. Sec. Council, *Doc. S/3179*.

[5] Lauterpacht, *Reports 1950*, Case No. 149: *The Flying Trader*, pp. 446–447.

[6] U.N. Sec. Council, *Off. Rec.*, 6th year, 555th meeting, p. 7; 9th year, 658th meeting, p. 31; 659th meeting, p. 23; 661st meeting, p. 17; 686th meeting, p. 21; 10th year, 688th meeting, p. 18.

in so far as they must be exercised in accordance with those provisions; in case the measures taken do not conform to them, they cannot be said to be either "reasonable" or "necessary." Article 11 of the Convention has bound Egypt not to take any measures, even for the defence of her territory, which shall "interfere with the free use of the Canal." In so far as some of the measures taken by Egypt on the occasion of the Palestinian War do, in fact, interfere with the free use of the Canal by all the nations of the world, they must be said to be contrary to the provisions of the Convention, and consequently neither "reasonable" nor "necessary."

The reaction of the international community to the Egyptian measures described above has been varied and, on the whole, rather mild. Whereas a few States have insisted on the rights of all nations to navigate the Canal,[1] others have emphasized the commercial aspects, leaving in the background the measures taken in time of war.[2] There has even been one State, at least, which has defended these very measures,[3] but the great majority of the international community have chosen to maintain a discreet silence. They would thus seem to have either readily acquiesced in the measures taken, or tacitly acknowledged that the Convention itself was for them nothing but a *res inter alios acta*.

From the survey just completed of the practice of States with regard to the Constantinople Convention several conclusions may be drawn:

First, there is no evidence to show that the Convention was regarded from the beginning by non-signatory States as an international settlement. Later practice of States would seem rather to point in the opposite direction. It cannot therefore be said that non-signatory States have become bound by the Constantinople Convention on account of its legal character as an international settlement.

Second, the survey also shows that there has been no uniformity in the practice followed. If the Convention has been, on the whole, well observed in time of peace[4] and even in time of war when the

---

[1] *Ibid.*, 6th year, 553rd meeting, p. 5 (Netherlands); 9th year, 686th meeting, p. 6 (Israel); 10th year, 688th meeting, p. 10 (New Zealand).

[2] *Ibid.*, 10th year, 687th meeting, pp. 9–10 (France); *The Suez Problem*, p. 148 (Ethiopia). The same could be said, perhaps, of many other nations, among which the United States and Great Britain should be included, in so far as their condemnation of the Egyptian measures was based on the fact that Egypt could not be considered a belligerent after the Armistice Agreement rather that on the fact that the measures were forbidden by the Constantinople Convention.

[3] China. See U.N. Sec. Council, *Off. Rec.*, 6th year, 553rd meeting, p. 11.

[4] The only violation of the freedom of passage would seem to have been the Egyptian

territorial sovereign was neutral,[1] it has bcen consistently violated when the sovereign was one of the belligerents. Thus, an essential element for the constitution of an international custom is missing.

Third, the second element required for an international custom, the *opinio necessitatis iuris*, is also missing. The fact that the international community has, by and large, acquiesced in the violations of the two World Wars and of the Palestinian War shows conclusively that the great majority of States do not feel themselves bound by the provisions of the Convention.

Fourth, it thus becomes absolutely clear that no customary rule of international law has grown up, whereby the Constantinople Convention has become binding on non-signatory States. Rather, the opposite conclusion may be drawn, namely, that even signatory States have acquiesced in a practical, though indefinite, revision of the Constantinople Convention.

Section IV   LEGAL CONSEQUENCES

The conclusions arrived at in the two previous sections concerning the legal effects of the Constantinople Convention give rise to certain important legal consequences, which must in turn be analyzed here.

The first legal consequence is that non-signatory States have never become parties to the Convention and consequently are not bound by its provisions, since neither tacit acceptance, nor international settlement, nor custom – the only methods known in international law for extending the provisions of a convention to third states – are applicable in the present case. It follows that Egypt is not bound *vis-à-vis* non-signatories to grant them the advantages of the Convention but only *vis-à-vis* signatory Powers, so that the former have no legal right to complain in case Egypt disregards some of the provisions of the Convention.[2]

A second and more important consequence is that, although Egypt and the signatory Powers are mutually bound by all the provisions of the Convention, still it cannot reasonably be held that Egypt is

Order of May 28, 1947, mentioned above on p. 84. In addition, there were also violations of the provisions on internationalization and demilitarization. See above, pp. 82–84.

[1] The last instance was the Ethiopian War of 1935–1936, during which the Canal was maintained open to Italian warships and military transports.

[2] This was the position taken by the Egyptian representative in the Security Council on Feb. 15, 1954. See *Off. Rec.*, 9th year, 659th meeting, p. 23.

bound, even *vis-à-vis* signatory Powers, to grant non-signatories all the advantages of the Convention without at the same time imposing on them all its obligations, for this would run contrary to the most elementary principles of international law. Such an obligation on the part of Egypt would, in fact, mean that she was bound to grant free passage through the Canal even to the vessels of those non-signatories with which she might be at war, while these same nations, not being bound by the Convention, would be free to attack the Canal if they chose. Such a one-sided obligation is inconceivable in the absence of a guaranty given by the signatory Powers. So long as non-signatories are not bound by the Convention, Egypt, as the territorial sovereign of the Canal, cannot be held to be bound to grant them free passage under all circumstances.[1] The Constantinople Convention forms an integrated whole, and its various provisions cannot be separated from each other to suit the preferences of the different States. If the signatory Powers imposed in 1888 the Constantinople Convention on Egypt as a permanent settlement, they must have done it on the understanding that either all other nations of the world would accede to the Convention, or at least, that they would, somehow, become bound by its provisions. Once this turns out not to be so, the whole structure built upon such a basis comes to the ground.

The third legal consequence, which would seem to follow from the previous one, is that in a war in which, at least, some of the belligerents are non-signatory Powers, Egypt, whether belligerent or neutral, would be free to take any measures which she might deem necessary to protect her interests as a belligerent or neutral power, even if this requires the temporary closure of the Canal to the vessels of some nations.

The fourth legal consequence is that with regard to signatory Powers, Egypt is bound by all the provisions of the Convention. However, as a result of the practice followed in the wars of 1914, 1939 and 1948, and acquiesced in, if not approved, by all concerned, when she, as the territorial sovereign of the Canal, is a belligerent, the Convention must be deemed suspended for the duration of the war, even if all the other belligerents are signatory Powers.

From the foregoing considerations a fifth and last consequence follows. Since Egypt is not bound by the provisions of the Conven-

---

[1] See the pertinent remarks made by Judges Anzilotti and Huber on this subject. P.C.I.J., *Ser. A*, No. 1 (1923), p. 39.

tion when she is a belligerent or when there is a war in which some of
the belligerents are non-signatories, neither she nor the Canal is, in
either case, protected by the provisions on neutralization of the
Convention. If Egypt is free to disregard the Convention, she cannot
at the same time claim the protection of its provisions. In these two
cases, the Canal is in no more privileged a position than any other
part of the Egyptian territory; consequently, the Canal has, in fact,
ceased to be neutralized.

In conclusion, it may be said by way of summary that first, the
Constantinople Convention is still binding on all the signatories, with
the possible exception of the case when Egypt is a belligerent. Second,
the Convention is not operative among non-signatories, but Egypt
is bound by its provisions to grant them free passage in time of peace.
Third, as a result of the "regime of internationality," all nations of
the world, whether signatories or non-signatories, always retain the
right to send through the Canal their merchant vessels in time of
peace.

This was the legal situation of the Suez Canal on July 26, 1956,
when President Nasser nationalized the Suez Canal Company. The
effects which such a nationalization might have had on the legal
regime of the Canal remain to be considered.

CHAPTER V

THE SUEZ CANAL SINCE 1956:
THE NATIONALIZED CANAL

The Presidential Decree of July 26, 1956, provided in its Article 1 that

"The Universal Company of the Suez Maritime Canal (Egyptian joint-stock company) is hereby nationalized. All its assets, rights and obligations are transferred to the Nation and all the organizations and committees that now operate its management are hereby dissolved.

"Stockholders and holders of founders' shares shall be compensated for the ordinary or founders shares they own in accordance with the value of the shares shown in the closing quotations of the Paris Stock Exchange on the day preceding the effective date of the present law."[1]

This unannounced Decree was followed within a week by the publication of a Tripartite Statement of August 2 in which the United States, Great Britain, and France jointly challenged President Nasser's right to nationalize the Canal Company on the following grounds:

"1...The Universal Suez Canal Company has always had an international character in terms of its shareholders, Directors and operating personnel...

"2...the present action involves far more than a simple act of nationalization. It involves the arbitrary and unilateral seizure by one nation of an international agency which has the responsibility to maintain and to operate the Suez Canal...

"3. They consider that the action taken by the Government of Egypt, having regard to all the attendant circumstances, threatens the freedom and security of the Canal as guaranteed by the Convention of 1888..."[2]

Before proceeding to an examination of the effects of nationalization on the legal regime of the Canal it becomes necessary to consider in detail the claims made by the Western Powers.

[1] *The Suez Problem*, p. 31.
[2] *Ibid.*, pp. 34–35.

Section I LEGAL CHARACTER OF THE CANAL COMPANY

The Universal Company of the Maritime Canal of Suez was officially established by the Second Concession of January 5, 1856. It was the Viceroy's wish that investors of all nations should subscribe to its shares in order to make it universal in fact as well as in name. Although that wish was not fully met at the beginning, it came close to realization when in 1875 Disraeli in the name of the British Government got control of 44% of the shares.[1] The universal character was also visible in the composition of its Board of Directors, in which different nationalities were at all times represented.[2] In addition, the statutes of the Company were approved by the Viceroy of Egypt and repeatedly modified by agreement with the Egyptian Government.[3] All these characteristics gave the Suez Canal Company a peculiar aspect, but neither any nor all all of them together were sufficient to endow it with a supra-national or international character, as claimed by some Powers at the London Conference of August 1956.[4]

The legal status of the Company was purposely made vague from the outset. Article 3 of the Company's statutes provided that "the Company has its seat at Alexandria and its administrative domicile in Paris,"[5] but nowhere was there to be found what this distinction implied. Article 73 further provided that

"The Company being organized, with the approval of the Egyptian Government, as a joint stock company, by analogy to the joint stock companies authorized by the French Government, is governed by the principles of these latter companies.
"Although having its company seat at Alexandria, the Company elects legal domicile and assignment of jurisdiction at its administrative domicile in Paris, where all writs must be served."

Finally, according to Article 74, all disputes between the shareholders, not settled by arbitrators named by the parties, should be taken before the Court of Appeal of Paris.

It was precisely on the base of these ill-defined provisions that Lesseps was able to claim immunity from French jurisdiction in 1872, in which he was strongly supported by the Sultan of Turkey,[6] and

---

[1] See above, p. 8.
[2] See above, p. 7, n. 5.
[3] See above, p. 5.
[4] Besides the Tripartite Statement, see Mr. Dulles's speech on August 16. *The Suez Problem*, p. 73. See also Watt, *Britain and the Suez Canal*, p. 25.
[5] *B.F.St. Pap.*, 55 (1864–1865) 976, Annex.
[6] *Doc. Dipl.*, Affaire du Canal de Suez (1881), p. 18.

three years later to assert that the Company was a French Company, under the jurisdiction of the French Consulate.[1]

However, the Convention of February 22, 1866, incorporated in the Sultan's *Firman* of March 19, categorically stated in its Article 16 that

"Inasmuch as the *Compagnie Universelle du Canal Maritime de Suez* is Egyptian, it is governed by the laws and customs of the country: however, as regards its constitution as a corporation and the relations of its partners with one another, it is, by a special Convention, governed by the laws which, in France, govern joint stock companies..."[2]

When, in 1872, the *Tribunal de commerce de la Seine* of Paris attempted to interpret a clause of the 1856 Concession, the Sultan of Turkey immediately protested by a telegram to the French Government asserting that

"la Compagnie universelle du canal maritime de Suez, dont le siège principal se trouve établi à Alexandrie, est égyptienne, et, comme elle, soumise aux lois et usages de l'Empire."[3]

and the French *Tribunal de Cassation* expressly recognized in its decision of February 23, 1874, regarding the same case, that the Suez Canal Company was not subject to French legislation in the matter of tonnage measurement.[4]

The Egyptian character of the Company, thus firmly established by official legislation, diplomatic action and judicial decisions, was further strengthened by the proclamation of Egypt as an independent and sovereign state in 1922. In a series of decisions, mainly concerning the interpretation of the monetary *franc*, referred to in the Concessions, as the gold *franc*, the mixed Court of Appeals of Alexandria laid emphasis on the Egyptian and universal character of the Company.[5] The decision of February 26, 1940, in the case of *Credit Alexandrin v. Cie Universelle du Canal Maritime de Suez*, may be taken as the definitive pronouncement of the Court on the legal character of the Company:

"D'après les actes de concession et les statuts, la nationalité égyptienne de la Compagnie du Canal de Suez ne saurait être l'objet d'une sérieuse contestation...

[1] *Parl. Pap.*, Egypt No. 2 (1876), C.1392, p. 130, No. 174.
[2] *The Suez Problem*, p. 15.
[3] *Doc. Dipl.*, Affaire du Canal de Suez (1881), p. 18.
[4] Sirey, *Recueil General des Lois et des Arrêts*, 1874, I, p. 150.
[5] *Bulletin de Législation et de Jurisprudence Egyptiennes*, 34 (1921–1922), Part II, pp. 162–163; 37 (1924–1925), Part II, pp. 470–1. *Recueil Dalloz*, 1924, p. 190. *Gazette des Tribunaux Mixtes d'Egypte*, 23 (1932–1933), p. 304.

"Tout en étant égyptienne de nationalité, cette Compagnie avait un carac-
tère universel, parce qu'elle devait s'adresser à différents pays pour réunir les
capitaux nécessaires pour l'entreprise, comme elle devait aussi avoir des rapports avec les compagnies de navigation de tous les pays du monde.

"Et il a été déjà définitivement jugé entre parties que cette société était à la
fois une société égyptienne et universelle, comme d'ailleurs l'indique son nom:
'Compagnie universelle du Canal maritime de Suez.'

"De cette double qualité de société à la fois égyptienne et universelle, il
résulte qu'il était naturel de choisir un étalon monétaire commun à plusieurs
pays."[1]

The conclusion then seems inescapable that the Suez Canal Company was in 1956 an Egyptian company subject in all respects to the
laws and customs of the country. That it also possessed a universal
character, in the sense just referred to, does not deprive it of its
Egyptian nationality, for as President Nasser aptly expressed it: "It
cannot be at the same time Egyptian and non-Egyptian or an
Egyptian and an international company, as this is contrary to the
principles of law."[2] It follows, that the first claim made by the
Western Powers in their tripartite Statement, to the effect that the
Suez Canal Company had an international character, must be rejected.

The second claim, made in the same Statement, expressed the
opinion that the Suez Canal Company was an international agency
which had the responsibility to maintain and to operate the Canal,
and consequently could not be nationalized. The fact that the Company was Egyptian could only mean, according to the interpretation
given by the French Prime Minister at the London Conference of
1956, that in the present organization of the world every international company is compelled to adopt, at least for its seat, "a national
character," but without losing by it its international function. And
he mentioned "as an example which is absolutely comparable to that
of the Suez Canal Company, that of the Bank of International Settlements, whose seat is...at Basle."[3]

The drafting of the claim, as well as of its interpretation, perhaps
betrays the haste with which those statements were made. No sufficient attention seems to have been paid at the time to the different
elements which were involved in the Suez question. An attempt,
therefore, will be made here to analyze the most important of them.

The first element, which, in a sense, controlled all others, was

[1] *Bull. de Légis. et de Jurisp. Egypt.*, 5 (1939–1940), Part II, pp. 186–187.
[2] Statement by President Nasser Rejecting Invitation to the London Conference,
August 12, 1956. *The Suez Problem*, p. 48.
[3] *Ibid.*, p. 89.

Egyptian sovereignty over the canal, which replaced the former Turco-Egyptian sovereignty that existed at the time the Concessions were granted. This sovereignty was not altered as a result of the Concessions of 1854 and 1856, nor was any part of it transferred to the Canal Company. The Viceroy of Egypt assuaged the fears, expressed on this matter by the Turkish Government, in a reply given in March 1855, in which he said,

"Il n'y aura lieu de réclamer de la Compagnie concessionnaire du canal des deux mers aucune garantie concernant la souveraineté territoriale, qui restera intacte en Turquie, lorsque des capitaux anonymes viendront s'engager dans une entreprise de voie de communication, au même titre que les capitaux nationaux ou étrangers au moyen desquels s'exécutent depuis longtemps, en Angleterre, en France et en Allemagne, des chemins de fer ou des canaux. Aucun de ces pays n'a jamais eu la pensée, en admettant des capitaux, de traiter avec les sociétés qui les représentent sur des intérêts de souveraineté locale qui, restant réservés, ne peuvent pas être mis en discussion et sont inaliénables."[1]

The same opinion was expressed by Lesseps five days only after the second Concession of January 5, 1856, was granted –

"La concession faite à une compagnie d'ouvrir et d'exploiter un passage à travers le territoire égyptien, avec déclaration de neutralité, ne *dénationalise* pas ce passage."[2]

Nine years later, the same Lesseps in a *Note sur la juridiction dans l'Isthme* to the French Ambassador in Constantinople stated categorically that Egyptian jurisdiction applied to all persons of any nationality working in the Canal, and added that

"Faut-il répéter que la Compagnie, uniquement commerciale, n'a aucun droit à donner ou à ôter au gouvernement égyptien, et qu'elle ne peut d'aucune manière apporter un changement à la condition légale ou usagère des étrangers et des indigènes dans leurs rapports judiciaires?"[3]

This situation was officially recognized in the Convention of February 22, 1866, Article 9 which read:

"The Maritime Canal and all its appurtenances shall remain under the jurisdiction of the Egyptian police, who shall operate freely as at any other point of the territory, so as to assure good order, public safety, and observance of the laws and regulations of the country."[4]

The same idea was expressed again in the Anglo-Egyptian Treaty of 1936 wich qualified the Suez Canal as "an integral part of Egypt."[5]

[1] Lesseps, *Lettres*, v. 1, pp. 150–151.
[2] *Ibid.*, p. 330.
[3] *Ibid.*, v. 5, pp. 96–97.
[4] *The Suez Problem*, p. 14.
[5] *L.N.T.S.*, 173 (1936–1937) 406: Art. 8.

The foregoing documents make it abundantly clear that Egyptian sovereignty over the Canal has always remained unimpaired, and consequently how rightly the Egyptian representative could claim in the Security Council in January 1955, that

"the Suez Canal lies in Egyptian territory; it is an integral part of Egypt and is subject to Egyptian sovereignty. The fact that the ports of Suez and Port Said are ports of access to the Canal does not alter the fact that they are Egyptian ports, under Egyptian sovereignty, and that the area of the territorial sea along their coasts is also under Egyptian sovereignty."[1]

A second element, intimately connected with that of sovereignty, was Egyptian property of the Canal. Article 10 of the 1854 Concession expressly provided that

"On the expiration of the concession, the Egyptian Government shall take the place of the company; it shall enjoy all its rights without reservation and shall enter into full possession of the canal between the two seas and all the establishments dependent thereon. An agreement reached amicably or by arbitration shall determine the compensation to be allotted to the company for the transfer of its equipment and movable property."[2]

And the 1856 Concession, in a still more explicit way, stated in its Article 16 that at the expiration of the 99 years period "the Egyptian Government will resume possession of the maritime canal constructed by the company,"[3] thereby making it clear that the property of the canal, as distinguished from that of the equipment and supplies for which alone compensation was to be paid, had always remained in the hands of the Egyptian Government, and that only its possession and use had been granted to the Company for the period of the concession.[4]

It was for this reason that the Turkish Government strongly protested in 1872 when Lesseps offered to the Powers the Canal for sale. In a letter of January 10 to the Ambassador in London, the Turkish Grand-Vizir stated categorically that

"the Sublime Porte could not admit, even in principle, the sale of the Canal or the creation of an International Administration on its own territory. On the other hand, M. de Lesseps, having only the concession of the undertaking, could never have the right of raising questions of such a nature."[5]

---

[1] U.N. Sec. Council, *Off. Rec.*, 10th year, 688th meeting, p. 20.
[2] *The Suez Problem*, p. 3.
[3] See Appendix A, below.
[4] See also Berkol, *Le Statut Juridique actuel des Portes Maritimes Orientales de la Méditerranée*, p. 319 and Sibert, *Traité de Droit International Public*, v. 1, p. 764, n. 3.
[5] *Parl. Pap.*, Egypt No. 2 (1876), C.1392, pp. 161–162.

In other words, the Canal was Egyptian property temporarily operated by an Egyptian company, which could never have the right to dispose of it.

The third element involved in the Suez question was the administration of the Canal. Different from sovereignty and property, administration implied only maintenance and operation of the undertaking. The Egyptian Government, as the territorial sovereign and sole owner of the Canal, might have decided to operate the Canal itself, either directly without the aid of any intermediaries, or indirectly through a public body or agency. Instead, it chose a different method, that of a concession to a company of investors of many nations.

Both the first Concession of 1854 and that of 1856 expressly empowered the concessionary company to construct the canal and to operate it for 99 years.[1] Article 17 of the latter Concession provided that

"In order to compensate the company for the expenses of construction, maintenance, and operation for which it is made responsible by these presents, we authorize it, henceforth and for its entire term of possession...to establish and collect, for passage in the canals and the ports belonging thereto, navigation, pilotage, towage, and anchorage fees..."

The Concessions, therefore, were grants made to the new company for the purpose of constructing and, later, operating the Canal; in other words, they put the company in charge of the administration of the Canal. There is no doubt that these Concessions, granted by the Egyptian Government and later confirmed by the Sultan of Turkey, were acts of internal government, which fell outside the range of activity of international law.[2] And by the same token, the Company established by those legal acts was, in spite of its name and the nationality of its shareholders, an Egyptian Company of a private character in charge of an Egyptian undertaking, and consequently subject in all respects to the laws of the country and to the jurisdiction of its legitimate Government.

The fourth element in the Suez question concerned the right of passage enjoyed by all nations. As a result of the regime of internationality established by the 1856 Concession, all nations of the world acquired the right to send through the Canal their merchant vessels

---

[1] See Concess. of 1854, Preamble and Arts. 1 and 3; Concess. of 1856, Arts. 1, 14, 15 and 16.
[2] See above, pp. 48 and 60–61.

in time of peace. The Constantinople Convention of 1888 enlarged this right, at least as far as the signatories were concerned, to include all kind of navigation whether in time of peace or in time of war.[1] The net result was to introduce in the Suez question an element of a different legal nature from that of the other three already mentioned, in so far as this last element was governed by international law. Failure to distinguish this different legal character on the part of many writers and statesmen, has been the source of much confusion and political misunderstanding.

It has been explained above how the regime of internationality came into being, and how this took place without transmuting the legal character of the 1856 Concession.[2] The Concession was an act of internal law by which a right was given to a private company to construct and operate the Canal. However, one Article of this Concession, namely Article 14, was used by the territorial sovereign to make an offer to the international community of a perpetual right of passage through the Canal. The Article in question was nothing but the instrument chosen by the sovereign to make his declaration. Such a use of the Article as the vehicle of a unilateral declaration could not possibly change its legal character, which was of internal law. On the other hand, the content of this same Article became, through diplomatic correspondence and action, the object of an international transaction between the territorial sovereign and the international community, performed not only outside of, but in addition to the internal transaction of the Concession. The legal character of the Concession, therefore, remained unimpaired, and the Company, as a party to that Concession, and to that alone, totally unaffected by the international transaction which had taken place without its intervention.

Thus from the beginning, there were two transactions around the Concession: one, of an internal character – the Concession itself – between the Egyptian Government and the Canal Company; another, of an international character – the unilateral declaration accepted by the nations – concluded between the Egyptian Government and the international community. Of the three parties to these transactions, the Egyptian Government was the only one that was at the same time a party to both. It thus became bound to maintain the Canal open by a double obligation: by Article 14 of the Concession it became bound *vis-à-vis* the Company, the obligation being of an

---

[1] See above, pp. 88–89.
[2] See above, pp. 60–61.

internal character; and by the same Article, as the object of the
international transaction, it became bound *vis-à-vis* the international community, the obligation being, in this case, of an international character. On the other hand the Company, which was only
a party to a transaction of internal law, was bound *vis-à-vis* the
Egyptian Government to maintain the Canal open to navigation, but
had neither rights nor obligations with regard to the international
community.

According to the Concession, the Company had been given the
responsibility to maintain and operate the Canal by the Egyptian
Government. This responsibility to act as the administrator of the
Canal remained unaffected by the international transaction. The
transaction did not make the Company an agency of the international community. Its only object was to secure a right of passage
from the Egyptian Government, independently from the administrator of the Canal whosoever he might be. Therefore, the Company
remained, as before, responsible, and solely responsible, to the Egyptian Government for the way it maintained and operated the Canal.

The four elements, just analyzed, involved in the Suez question
were not always sharply distinguished in actual practice. It thus came
to pass that the legal effects of the international regime of navigation,
which were of an international character, were quite often ascribed
to some of the other three elements, all of which had an internal
character. As a result of this misunderstanding, the Canal Company
acquired in the eyes of many statesmen and writers a position com-
parable to that of an international agency in charge of an international function.

To this way of thinking Lesseps himself might have greatly con-
tributed, for he never seems to have realized the exact nature of the
Company[1] or the role it was supposed to play with regard to the
Canal.[2] Another contributory factor was the purchase of the shares

[1] In 1874 Lesseps refused to accept the decision of the Constantinople Conference
of 1873 on tonnage measurement, and the Viceroy of Egypt was compelled to send
on April 29 a military force of 10.000 men to take possession of the Canal if the
Company persisted in its opposition. See Hallberg, *The Suez Canal*, p. 227. Again in
1875, the Company refused to receive judicial documents through the medium of the
local authorities, which provoked a sharp reply from the Egyptian Minister. See
Parl. Pap., Egypt No. 2 (1876), C.1392, p. 129.

[2] See for instance his remarks in 1860 concerning the neutrality of the Canal, when
he asserts that "la Compagnie est prête à s'associer à tous les efforts de la politique,"
Lesseps, *Lettres*, v. 3, p. 295; or the Resolution passed by the Council of the Company
in 1882 on the occasion of the landing of British troops in the Canal: "Le maintien
de cette neutralité ...constitue pour la Compagnie une obligation qui est la base de
sa Concession." *Parl. Pap.*, Egypt No. 17 (1882), C.3391, Inclosure in No. 579.

by Disraeli in 1875, as a result of which the Government of a Great Power became officially not only a shareholder, but the strongest shareholder of the company, controlling 44% of all the shares.[1] A third factor was, undoubtedly, the absence of political independence in Egypt for many years after the Concessions were granted, and the fact that Turkey, the suzerain, was a weak country and diplomatically subservient to the wishes of the European Powers. This led those Powers to believe that they had a right to manage the affairs of the Canal,[2] and the Company to act as if it were an independent entity, protected by the powerful influence of France.[3] The last factor was the Constantinople Convention of 1888, concluded at the wish of the Great Powers, in which express reference was made to the Concessions and to the Company.[4]

In view of the foregoing precedents, it is quite understandable that the three Western Powers might have thought in 1956 that the Egyptian Nationalization Decree of July 26 violated vested international rights by the mere fact of taking over the Canal Company.

The second claim made in the Tripartite Statement, quoted above, purported to give to the Company the status of "an international agency," which had the responsibility to maintain and to operate the Suez Canal. The letter of September 12, 1956, from the representatives of France and the United Kingdom to the Security Council spoke of "the system of international operation of the Suez Canal,"[5] and the French Prime Minister specified that it was an "international public service."[6]

The claim was based on two different grounds: first, the regime that prevailed in the Canal before 1888; and second, the Constantinople Convention of that year.

According to the opinion expressed by the Prime Minister of France in the Security Council, the principle of free passage written into the 1856 Concession did not have before 1888 "any international

---

[1] See above, p. 8.
[2] See for instance some of the remarks made by the delegates at the Paris Commission of 1885. The German delegate: "The Company has never done anything without the assent of the powers." The Austro-Hungarian delegate "sees in this interference by Europe, brought about by the Company, a recognition of the public and international character of the undertaking." *Parl. Pap.*, Egypt No. 19 (1885), C.4599, pp. 197 and 201.
[3] See above, p. 98, n. 1.
[4] See below, pp. 100–102.
[5] U.N. Sec. Council, *Doc. S/3645*.
[6] Statement on August 17 at the London Conference of 1956. *The Suez Problem*, p. 87.

guarantee other than the Company's universal character."[1] This was, as the British Foreign Minister asserted, "the 19th century way of doing what today we should do by means of an inter-governmental international regime."[2] In other words, the Canal had been "internationalized," and the Company, because of its universal character, was the agency selected by the international community to maintain and operate the waterway.

In view of what has been said in the preceding pages about the way in which the international regime of navigation was established on the Canal and the role that the Company was to play as the administrator of the undertaking, the position held by France and the United Kingdom is absolutely untenable and need not further be discussed here. The Company was, from the outset, a private Egyptian company put by the Egyptian Government in charge of the administration of the Canal, but entirely alien to the international regime established in it.

The second ground on which the Western claim was based concerned the reference made in the Constantinople Convention to the Viceroy's Concessions.

The Preamble to the 1888 Convention expressed the purpose as being to establish

"by a Conventional Act, a definitive system intended to guarantee, at all times and to all the Powers, the free use of the Suez Maritime Canal, and thus to complete the system under which the navigation of this canal has been placed by the Firman of His Imperial Majesty the Sultan, dated February 22, 1866, and sanctioning the Concessions of His Highness the Khedive."[3]

The American Secretary of State, at the first London Conference of 1956, argued that "the decree of February 22, 1866...has been by reference incorporated into and made part of what is called the definite system set up by the 1888 treaty."[4]

And the representative of Belgium took the position at the Security Council that the word "to complete," referred to in the Preamble, was designed

"to establish a close and unquestionable connexion between the act of concession establishing the Company and the Convention affirming, at the international level, the principle of freedom of navigation, with the inevitable

---

[1] U.N. Sec. Council, *Off. Rec.*, 11th year, 735th meeting, p. 19.
[2] *Ibid.*, p. 4.
[3] See Appendix B, below.
[4] *The Suez Problem*, p. 73.

consequence that the Company and the system which it safeguards cannot be destroyed without violating the Convention."[1]

This conclusion, strange though it may seem, has been accepted by a number of contemporary writers, who assert that the Company's "rights and privileges could not be repealed unilaterally because they had received international sanction in the preamble to the 1888 Convention."[2] This is another instance of the misunderstanding created by the confusion of the four elements of which mention has been made above.

What the Preamble intends "to complete" is not "the act of concession establishing the Company," as the Belgian representative claimed, but "the system under which the navigation of this canal has been placed by the *Firman* of...the Sultan." Now, the system of navigation established on the Canal as a result of the Concessions was the "regime of internationality," derived from an international transaction the object of which was Article 14 of the 1856 Concession.[3] It was in this sense, and in this sense only, that the Sultan's *Firman* sanctioning the 1856 Concession did establish an international system of navigation in the Canal, which the Constantinople Convention of 1888 intended "to complete," and to which reference is made in the Preamble.

Even if, for the sake of argument, the possibility were contemplated that the reference in the Preamble was concerned with the Concession itself, the only possible conclusion would be that the Preamble took note of the fact that the Company was in charge of the administration of the Canal by a decision of the Egyptian Government, which had granted the Concessions; but never that the Concessions had acquired by that reference an international character, nor that the Company had been transmuted into an international agency whose status could not be modified by the same Government which created it.[4]

The same conclusion is borne out by Article 14 of the 1888 Convention, which separates definitely the newly established international regime of navigation, which is supposed to be perpetual, from the duration of the Acts of Concession of the Canal Company.[5] If it were

---

[1] U.N. Sec. Council, *Off. Rec.*, 11th year, 737th meeting, p. 25.
[2] Avram, *op. cit.*, p. 33 and writers mentioned therein.
[3] See above, pp. 97–98.
[4] See Statement by the representative of Egypt in the Security Council. *Off. Rec.*, 11th year, 736th meeting, p. 7.
[5] Statement by President Nasser Rejecting Invitation to the London Conference. *The Suez Problem*, p. 48.

argued, again, that such a reference to the duration of the Concessions implied a recognition of their life-limit, the answer would simply be that the Powers, which concluded the Convention, took most probably that limit for granted, but it would not follow that they had entered into a binding engagement for the purpose of preventing the territorial sovereign from revoking those Concessions.

It must then be concluded that the Company had not been incorporated into the 1888 Convention as a result of the reference made to the Concessions in the Preamble to that Treaty. Consequently, the second claim put forward in the Tripartite Statement, concerning the status of the Company as an international agency which had the responsibility to maintain and operate the Canal, must also be rejected.[1]

The only conclusion to be drawn from this Section is that the Canal Company, whatever its name and its importance, was purely a private Egyptian company subject in all respects to the laws of the country and to the jurisdiction of the Egyptian Government. As such, it was also subject to nationalization in the same way as any other Egyptian enterprise,[2] provided, however, that the *minimum standard* required by international law for the protection of aliens was fully met. Article 1, paragraph 2, of the Nationalization Decree of 1956, providing for pecuniary compensation,[3] more than met that standard.[4] From this viewpoint therefore the nationalization of the Suez Canal Company by President Nasser must be held to have been both legal and valid.

However, there always remains the possibility that the nationalization of the Company, though legal in itself, might have affected the rights enjoyed by all nations to navigate the Canal, as the Company was in fact the administrator of that waterway. It thus becomes necessary to inquire into the effects of that act on the regime of the Canal.

---

[1] See letter of 17 Sept. 1956 from the representative of Egypt to the President of the Security Council. *Doc. S/3650.*

[2] See *Avis du Conseil d'Etat égyptien* of May 1883, where the *Conseil* speaks of the "droit intrinsèque de l'Etat dans les questions d'utilité publique" as a permanent reservation to the monopoly enjoyed by Lesseps to construct the Canal. *J.D.I.P.,* 10 (1883) 321.

[3] See above, p. 90.

[4] Visscher, *op. cit.* See also the conclusions reached by Isi Foighel on the present state of international law regarding the necessity of compensation in case of nationalization, in his recent monograph *Nationalization, A Study in the Protection of Alien Property in International Law,* p. 85.

Section II   EFFECTS OF NATIONALIZATION ON THE LEGAL
REGIME OF THE CANAL

The Tripartite Statement of August 2, 1956, in its third paragraph expressed the belief that the action taken by the Government of Egypt in nationalizing the Canal Company "having regard to all the attendant circumstances, threatens the freedom and security of the Canal as guaranteed by the Convention of 1888."[1] To which President Nasser replied that there was "no relation whatsoever between the Egyptian Suez Canal Company and the 1888 agreement concerning the freedom of navigation through the canal."[2]

The legal situation around the Suez Canal was dependent on a number of elements, or "attendant circumstances" as the three Powers expressed it, of which the most important were three: sovereignty, administration, and regime of navigation. The three elements were inter-related, in so far as they formed part of one legal situation – the Suez Canal question.

Historically, sovereignty over the Canal had been divided since 1841 between the Government of Egypt and the Ottoman Empire, though in a rather vague way.[3] The British military occupation of Egypt in 1882 altered the existing situation and caused sovereignty to be thenceforth split *de facto*, if not *de iure*, among three Governments. This state of affairs lasted until December 1914, when a British Protectorate over Egypt was proclaimed, which was subsequently recognized by Turkey in the Treaty of Lausanne of 1923.[4] Although Egypt was granted independence in 1922, she did not legally obtain full sovereignty over the Suez Canal until the Anglo-Egyptian Treaty of 1936.[5] British troops, however, remained in the Canal Zone Base, and were not withdrawn from the country until the new Anglo-Egyptian Treaty of 1954 was signed, through which Egypt regained, at last, full control in fact, as well as in law, over the Canal, as the only legitimate sovereign of the whole country.[6]

The evolution of the element of sovereignty, since the time of the Concessions, shows a trend toward the elimination of intermediaries and the centralization of all powers in the Egyptian Government.

[1] *The Suez Problem*, p. 35.
[2] Statement Rejecting Invitation to the London Conference, August 12. *Ibid.*, p. 50.
[3] See above, p. 5, n. 1.
[4] *B.F.St. Pap.*, 117 (1923) 543.
[5] *L.N.T.S.*, 173 (1936–1937) 406.
[6] *U.N.T.S*, 210 (1955) 24.

Matters pertaining to navigation in the Canal, which in the past had been handled by the Great Powers with the willing acquiescence of the Ottoman Empire, were to be settled in the future by direct agreement between the international community, on the one hand, and the Egyptian Government on the other, both acting on a basis of perfect parity.

The second element in the legal situation concerning the Canal was the right of passage enjoyed by all nations. This right was based on the regime of internationality established by the Concessions and later supplemented by the 1888 Convention. Since, according to the conclusions reached at the end of chapter IV, the Convention of Constantinople did not apply to non-signatories so as to grant them valid rights, the regime of internationality must be held to have remained in force for them.[1] For signatory Powers, the Convention is the only valid instrument, though with certain modifications introduced by the practice of States.[2] Egypt, in addition, as a party to the Convention, is bound *vis-à-vis* signatory States to grant to non-signatories free passage at least for their warships in time of peace.[3]

The third element in the complex legal situation concerned the administration of the Canal. From the outset, this administration had been in the hands of the Canal Company, established by the Concessions of the Viceroy of Egypt. Although the Company, being Egyptian, was solely responsible to the Egyptian Government and had neither rights nor obligations with regard to the international community, in fact, it was in contact with such a community in more than one way, and had to act, quite often, as an intermediary between it and the Egyptian Government. Article 17 of the 1856 Concession authorized the Company for the entire term of its administration

"to establish and collect...navigation, pilotage, towage, and anchorage fees, according to rate-schedules which it may change at any time, subject to the express condition that it shall:
 (1) Collect these fees without exception or favor from all vessels, under the same terms
 (2) Publish the rate-schedules three months before they become effective...
 (3) Not exceed for the special navigation fee the maximum figure of ten francs per ton of burden for vessels and ten francs a head for passengers."

---

[1] The Egyptian representative maintained in the Security Council on October 8, 1956, that "the system existing before the 1888 Convention was completely absorbed by that Convention." See *Off. Rec.*, 11th year, 736th meeting, p. 7. For the reasons expressed in the text this opinion cannot be accepted.
[2] See above, pp. 87–89.
[3] *Ibid.*

This Article providing for a ceiling in the Canal tolls became, in fact, a guarantee for the international community. The interest of the Canal Company lay in having the greatest possible number of vessels pass through the Canal, and consequently, in keeping the tolls as low as was necessary to attain that end. This, undoubtedly, coincided with the interest of the international community to navigate as freely and as cheaply as possible through the Canal. Such a coincidence of interests became, in fact, a guarantee for the international community, for it meant that, even if the Egyptian Government were to allow the Company to exact in the future higher tolls, the Company would never take advantage of that opportunity. And, as a matter of fact, before 1956 the Company had repeatedly decreased its toll-rates in times of prosperity.[1] This was, then, one way in which the Company, as the administrator of the Canal, came into contact with the international community.

Another way, though perhaps not as direct, was the limited protection given to the international community by the mere existence of the Company against the possibility of Egyptian political interference in the navigation of the Canal. It is quite true that the Company, being Egyptian, was subject to the laws and regulations made by Egypt, and it is equally true that the existence of the Company before 1956 did not prevent the Egyptian Government from enforcing its regulations against Israeli shipping, after the Armistice Agreement of 1949.[2] And yet, it cannot be denied that the mere presence of the Company in the Canal meant for the Egyptian Government a permanent obstacle in case it would be tempted to interfere actively in the navigation of the Canal. In this sense, too, the Company came into contact with the international community and acted as a *de facto* intermediary between it and the Egyptian Government.

Thus, the Company as the administrator of the Canal became by 1956 one of the three elements of the Suez question, playing the role of the sole remaining intermediary between the other two.[3] Such an element, though important, was not essential for the maintenance of the international regime, and consequently, could be altered or suppressed altogether by the Egyptian Government, to which the Company was in all respects subject, without necessarily altering or suppressing that regime. In so far, however, as the Company was

---

[1] See Reymond, *Histoire de la Navigation dans le Canal de Suez*, pp. 248–249.
[2] See above, pp. 85–86.
[3] See above, pp. 103–104,

"in fact," if not in law, connected with that regime, there was always the possibility that its suppression might alter "in fact" the regime of navigation and thus affect the rights already vested in the international community. A sharp rise in the toll-rates, after the Egyptian Government took over the Canal Company, might have considerably decreased the number of vessels passing through the Canal, or even stopped navigation altogether. This would have resulted in serious injury to the rights of the international community. From this view point, therefore, the suppression of the Canal Company could not be carried out, without previous consultation with the interested parties.[1]

As a result of the foregoing considerations, the nationalization of the Suez Canal Company, though perfectly legal in itself, must be deemed to have been carried out illegally, in so far as no provision was made beforehand, by mutual agreement between Egypt and the international community, to safeguard the rights of navigation of the latter in the Suez Canal. In other words, the nationalization of the Company was legal, but the way in which it was carried out was illegal; which, of course, made the whole act, also, internationally illegal.

In order to reach this conclusion, it is not necessary to show that the act of nationalization did in fact jeopardize the international regime of navigation in the Canal. It is enough to show that nationalization "might" have affected the existing regime, and that no previous understanding had been reached with the international community in order to offset that possible effect. This, it is believed, has been shown in the previous pages. The conclusion, then, must be that the nationalization of the Suez Canal Company in 1956 was simply illegal.[2]

Whether, in addition, the nationalization did in fact alter the existing regime depends entirely on the efficacy of the measures taken by President Nasser to guarantee freedom of navigation. To this inquiry the third and last section will be devoted.

---

[1] See above, p. 45.

[2] This conclusion is concerned exclusively with the legal aspect of the problem, and there is no intention whatsoever to pass judgment on the political aspects of the question. Whether President Nasser would have been able to discuss quietly the question of nationalization with the interested countries before it took place, is a question which might interest the future historian, but over which there is no way of giving a definite opinion at the present time. The morality therefore of the act, as distinguished from the mere legality, must remain for the time being a moot question.

Section III   LEGAL GUARANTEES CONCERNING THE
                INTERNATIONAL REGIME

The assertion was made in the previous section that the nationalization of the Company did not necessarily imply an alteration of the
regime of navigation in the Canal. The Tripartite Statement of
August 2 ,1956, considered, however, that "having regard to all the
attendant circumstances," that act threatened the freedom and security of the Canal.[1] On August 5, the same Powers proposed to establish
an *International Authority for the Suez Canal* whose purpose would
be to take over the operation of the Canal, ensuring Egypt an
equitable return.[2] The same proposal, under the name of *Suez Canal
Board*, was made at the end of the first London Conference,[3] and,
when this was rejected by President Nasser,[4] a second London Conference decided to establish a *Suez Canal Users Association*, whose
purpose would be "to assist the members in the exercise of their
rights as users of the Suez Canal," and "to promote safe, orderly,
efficient and economical transit"through it.[5]

There is little doubt that such proposals might have safeguarded
the rights of the international community and ensured an efficient
administration, but there is also no doubt that their acceptance would
have amounted to the establishment of a regime of internationalization in the Suez Canal. This the Western Powers had no right to do.
As members of the international community they enjoyed the right
of navigation through the Canal, and were entitled to take the
measures necessary to defend that right. This right, however, had
been granted by the territorial sovereign, and could not be altered
or enlarged, except with its consent. Egypt, on the other hand, was
bound to respect the rights which she had granted, but otherwise
could not be forced to enlarge those rights, even if this would result
in greater facilities for the international community.

The proposals, therefore, were based on a misconception of the
true legal character of the Suez Canal and of the rights of the international community over it.[6] Besides, there was absolutely no need of
such a regime of internationalization in order to ensure the free nav-

[1] See above, p. 103.
[2] *The Suez Problem*, p. 44.
[3] *Ibid.*, p. 291.
[4] *Ibid.*, p. 317.
[5] *Ibid.*, p 365.
[6] See e.g. the remarks made by the representative of New Zealand at the first
London Conference. *Ibid.*, pp. 204 and 206.

igation in the Canal, as was clearly shown by the Resolution of the Security Council of October 13, 1956, which met with general approval on the part of the international community.[1]

The Resolution adopted six principles as the basic requirements for any settlement of the Suez question, providing, among other things, for freedom of navigation without discrimination, insulation of the operation of the Canal from politics, and the fixing of tolls by agreement between Egypt and the users. This Resolution, which was basically accepted by Egypt,[2] made it clear in its simplicity that a compromise could easily be agreed upon, which, while respecting Egyptian sovereignty over the Canal, would also ensure the rights of navigation of the international community.

Unfortunately, before such an agreement had been worked out, the Anglo-French invasion of Egypt had left the Canal out of order. By the time it was reopened, the Egyptian Government had unilaterally established its own guarantees to ensure freedom of navigation in the Canal, which are, in fact, still in force.[3]

By the Declaration of April 24, 1957, the Egyptian Government reaffirmed its determination to uphold the Constantinople Convention of 1888, and, specifically, the provisions on freedom of navigation. It gave assurance that the Canal tolls would remain substantially the same as before, and made provision for partial negotiation with regard to them. Disputes with the signatories of the Constantinople Convention concerning its provisions would be referred to the International Court of Justice. Lastly, the Declaration was registered with the Secretariat of the United Nations, and declared to be an international instrument.

This Declaration does not include all of the six principles adopted by the Security Council. There is specifically no provision in it for insulating the operation of the Canal from politics, and the stipulation on tolls falls short of the principle embodied in the Resolution. On the other hand, the Declaration maintains the *status quo ante*, and goes, perhaps, even a little further in the direction of making the international community take some part in the fixing of toll-rates. Therefore, the Declaration is, in fact, a sufficient guaranty that the international regime of the Suez Canal, as it existed before the nationalization Decree, will be preserved.

---

[1] U.N. Sec. Council, *Doc. S/3675*. See also Appendix C, below.
[2] *Ibid., Doc. S/3728*.
[3] *Ibid., Doc. S/3818*. See also Appendix D, below.

However, the Declaration is a unilateral act of the Egyptian Government. In accordance with the opinion expounded above,[1] and specially, in view of the official registration of the document with the Secretariat of the United Nations, there can be little doubt that the Declaration is a true international instrument binding on Egypt, which cannot be unilaterally altered or revoked any more.[2] From this viewpoint the international regime of navigation in the Canal is sufficiently assured.

But the whole point is, precisely, that the Declaration could not be unilateral. The guaranty to maintain the international regime is not a favour or a grant made by the Egyptian Government of its own free will, but a right which the international community may, at the present time, demand from Egypt. The Declaration, therefore, in order to be a valid international instrument for solving the Suez question, should have been in the nature of a bilateral accord. In so far as the Declaration of April 24, 1957, did not fulfill this requirement, it must be considered, for the purpose for which it was intended, as internationally illegal.

This original illegality of the Declaration may subsequently be corrected, if the international community accepts the instrument as a fair, if temporary, solution of the problem. Such seems to have been the case with the present Declaration.

In the discussion which took place at the Security Council on April 26 and 27, the Declaration was considered by several countries as a sufficient and final settlement of the Suez question.[3] On the other hand, France and the United Kingdom, assailed the Declaration as insufficient and "in flagrant contradiction with the six principles" approved by the Security Council.[4] In between these extreme positions, the representative of the United States expressed what was probably the view of the great majority of the international community, when he said that "perhaps no final judgment can be made regarding the regime proposed by Egypt until it has been tried out in practice."[5] This amounts to a temporary acceptance of the new

[1] See above, pp. 27–29.
[2] See Letter of 26 April 1957 from the Secretary–General to the Minister for Foreign Affairs of Egypt. U.N. Sec. Council,*Doc. S/3819.* See also the assurances given by the representative of Egypt in the Security Council on April 26. *Off. Rec.,* 12th year, 777th meeting, pp. 21–22, para. 101.
[3] U.N. Sec. Council, *Off. Rec.,* 12th year, 776th meeting, p. 14 (Philippines), and 777th meeting, p. 12 (U.S.S.R.).
[4] *Ibid.,* 777th meeting, p. 20 (U.K.). See also the Communiqué of the Council of Ministers of France of May 15, 1957. *Doc. S/3829.*
[5] *Off. Rec.,* 776th meeting, p. 3, para. 11.

system by the international community, in which even France and the United Kingdom seem to have acquiesced later.[1] As a result, the Declaration of April 24, 1957, has become legal, and consequently must be taken as an acceptable, though perhaps only temporary,[2] solution of the complex Suez question.

[1] See Letter of 13 June 1957 from the Representative of France to the Secretary-General, in which the French Government declares that French ships will be allowed to use the Suez Canal. *Doc. S/3839/Rev. 1.*

[2] The U.S. representative remarked at the 776th meeting of the Security Council that "any *de facto* acquiescence by the United States must be provisional, and we reserve the right to express ourselves further on this matter in the future." *Off. Rec.,* 12th year, 776th meeting, p. 3.

Conclusion: The Future

At the end of this study on the international character of the Suez Canal, there is one feature that has come out more than once in the previous pages, which deserves particular attention: the unsettled condition of the Suez question. ·

At the present time, the regime that prevails in the Suez Canal is governed by the unilateral Egyptian Declaration of April 24, 1957, which embodies the Constantinople Convention of 1888. As already mentioned in the previous chapter, the Declaration has not been accepted as a permanent solution by the international community, but only as a temporary measure, which needs to be tested before it can be adopted as a final regime.

With regard to the future, there are two possibilities open. It may be that after some years the international community either expressly or tacitly accepts the Declaration as a permanent and equitable solution of the Suez question. The regime so established would not materially differ from the one that prevailed in the Canal before nationalization took place. Such a solution, however, as it must already be clear from the conclusions reached in this study, would leave unsolved the many problems that have accumulated during the history of the Canal and have never received an answer. The question of the revision of the Constantinople Convention and of its applicability to non-signatories are specific matters which urgently require to be settled. Therefore, this solution, though easy to be put in practice, would not seem to offer the best prospects for a permanent settlement of the Suez question in the future.

The second possibility open to the international community consists in a re-evaluation of the whole Suez question, made in agreement with Egypt as the territorial sovereign, which would take into account not only the old problems that need to be permanently settled but also the new changes brought about in the life of the international community.

Such a re-evaluation could take place either through a Treaty concluded between Egypt and a few Powers, as representatives of the international community, or still better, in a General Conference, convened under the auspices of the United Nations, to which each and every one of the nations of the world would be invited to attend, and which would agree on a comprehensive Convention where all outstanding problems regarding navigation in the Canal would be settled.

Among these problems, three seem to stand out as the most in need of a prompt solution: the revision of the Constantinople Convention, the question of the method for fixing tolls, and the settlement of disputes regarding the interpretation or application of the new Convention.

As it has been pointed out in chapter IV, the Constantinople Convention is in urgent need of revision. A number of provisions dealing with the equivalent of a regime of internationalization have become outmoded and are no longer valid. The regime of neutralization, which had a meaning within a framework of universal participation in the Convention, is not applicable today for non-signatory States. Even for the States which are parties to that Convention, the provisions on neutralization have lost much of their efficacy as a result of the changes brought about by the practice of States and by the acquisition of full statehood by Egypt, with which many of those provisions are incompatible.

The present inapplicability of many provisions of the Convention creates, in turn, a number of new problems which need to be faced and solved by the international community. Among them the question of freedom of navigation in case of war, when Egypt is one of the belligerents, appears at the present time as the most important of them all. This question is tied up with the problem of the legality of war under the Charter of the United Nations, and cannot therefore be entirely solved except in that wide framework.

Another question in need of a solution is the method for fixing tolls. Although in itself a privilege of the territorial sovereign, the fixing of tolls may affect the rights of navigation enjoyed by the nations of the world. It should therefore prove possible to devise a method whereby both the rights of the territorial sovereign and those of the international community could be reconciled.

Lastly, there is the problem of disputes with regard to navigation in the Canal, and the interpretation of the provisions of the new Convention. The only sensible solution would seem to be the acceptance of the compulsory jurisdiction of the International Court of Justice as an essential part of the Convention, so that all the nations of the world would be bound by it so long as they intend to use the Suez Canal.

If a Convention based on the broad principles outlined above is agreed upon, and its acceptance, through the signature and ratification of the instrument, is made compulsory as a necessary precondition for the use of the Canal, the so-called Suez question, it is believed, could once and for all be solved, and the regime of navigation through that important waterway be permanently assured for the good of the international community.

APPENDIX A

Act of Concession of the Viceroy of Egypt, and Terms and conditions for the Construction and Operation of the Suez Maritime Canal and Appurtenances. Alexandria, January 5, 1856.*

We, Mohammed Said Pasha, Viceroy of Egypt.

In view of our Act of Concession dated November 30, 1854, by which we gave to our friend, Mr. Ferdinand de Lesseps, exclusive power for the purpose of establishing and directing a universal company to cut through the Isthmus of Suez, to operate a passage suitable for large vessels, to establish or adapt two adequate entrances, one on the Mediterranean, the other on the Red Sea, and to establish one or two ports:

Mr. Ferdinand de Lesseps having represented to us that, in order to establish the aforementioned company in the form and under the conditions generally adopted for companies of this nature, it is desirable to stipulate in advance, in a more detailed and more complete act, on the one hand, the responsibilities, obligations, and charges to which such company will be subject and, on the other hand, the concessions, immunities, and advantages to which it shall be entitled, as well as the facilities that will be granted to it for its administration.

We have laid down as follows the conditions for the concession which forms the subject of these presents.

Obligations

Art. I. The company founded by our friend, Mr. Ferdinand de Lesseps, by virtue of our grant of November 30, 1854, must execute at its own expense, risk, and peril, all work, including construction, necessary for the establishment of:

(1) A canal for large seagoing vessels, between Suez on the Red Sea and the Bay of Pelusium in the Mediterranean Sea;

(2) An irrigation canal also suitable for use by Nile shipping, connecting the river with the maritime canal above–mentioned;

(3) Two irrigation and feeder branches leading off from the above-mentioned canal and flowing in the two directions of Suez and Pelusium.

The work will be carried out so as to be finished within a period of six years, except in the event of hindrances and delays resulting from *force majeure*.

II. The company shall be empowered to carry out the work with which it is charged by itself under State supervision or to cause it to be carried out by contractors through competitive bids or on an agreed-price basis. In all cases at least four-fifths of the workmen employed in this work are to be Egyptians.

* English translation from United States Departement of State, *The Suez Canal Problem*, pp. 4–9.

III. The canal suitable for large seagoing vessels shall be dug to the depth and width fixed by the program of the International Scientific Commission.

In conformity with this program it shall start from the port of Suez itself; it shall use the basin known as the Bitter Lakes Basin and Lake Timsa; it shall have its outlet in the Mediterranean, at a point on the Bay of Pelusium to be determined in the final plans to be drawn up by the company's engineers.

IV. The irrigation canal suitable for river shipping under the conditions of the said program shall begin near the city of Cairo, follow the valley (wadi) of Tumilat (ancient land of Goshen) and meet the large maritime canal at Lake Timsa.

V. The branches of the said canal are to lead off from it above the outlet into Lake Timsa; from that point they will be made to flow in the one case toward Suez and in the other case toward Pelusium, parallel to the large maritime canal.

VI. Lake Timsa will be converted into an inland port capable of receiving vessels of the largest tonnage.

The company will be bound, moreover, if necessary: (1) to construct a harbor at the point where the maritime canal enters the Bay of Pelusium; (2) to improve the port and roadstead of Suez, so as also to afford shelter to vessels there.

VII. The maritime canal and ports belonging to it, as well as the canal connecting with the Nile and the lead-off canal, shall at all times be kept in good condition by the company, at its expense.

VIII. Owners of riparian property wishing their land to be irrigated by water from the canals constructed by the company may obtain permission from it for this purpose through payment of compensation or a fee the amount of which shall be fixed by the conditions of Art. XVII hereinafter mentioned.

IX. We reserve the right to appoint at the administrative headquarters of the company a special commissioner, whose salary shall be paid by it, and who will represent with its administration the rights and interests of the Egyptian Government for the execution of the provisions of these presents.

If the company's administrative headquarters is established elsewhere than in Egypt, the company shall have itself represented at Alexandria by a superior agent vested with all powers necessary to see to the proper functioning of the service and the company's relations with our government.

Concessions

X. In return for the construction of the canals and appurtenances mentioned in the foregoing articles the Egyptian Government allows the company, without tax or fee, to enjoy the use of all such land, not belonging to private parties, as may be necessary.

It also allows it to enjoy the use of all now uncultivated land not belonging to private parties, which will be irrigated and cultivated by its efforts and at its expense, with this difference: (1) That the portions of land included in this last category shall be exempt from all taxes for ten years only, dating from their connection with the undertaking; (2) That after that period, and until the expiration of the concession, they shall be subject to the obligations and taxes to which the land of the other Egyptian provinces is subject under the same circumstances; (3) That the company can, subsequently, acting itself or through its assigns, retain the right to enjoy possession of this land and of the water-supply facilities necessary for its fertilization, subject to payment to the Egyptian Government of the taxes levied upon land under the same conditions.

XI. To determine the extent and limits of the land granted to the company, under the conditions of (1) and (2) of Article X above, reference is made to the plans annexed hereto, it being understood that on the said plans the lands granted for the construction of the canals and appurtenances free of tax or fee in conformity with (1) are shown in black, and the lands granted for cultivation through payment of certain fees in conformity with (2) are shown in blue.

All acts executed subsequent to our act of November 30, 1854 shall be considered null and void if they would result in creating for private parties as against the company either rights to compensation which did not exist at the time with respect to those lands, or rights to compensation that are more extensive than those which they were able to claim at that time.

XII. The Egyptian Government will make over to the Company, if desirable, privately-owned land the possession of which may be necessary to the execution of the work and the exploitation of the concession, provided the company pay fair compensation to the owners.

Compensation for temporary occupation or for definitive expropriation shall be settled amicably in so far as possible; in case of disagreement, it shall be fixed by a court of arbitration acting in summary proceedings and composed of: (1) an arbitrator chosen by the company; (2) an arbitrator chosen by the interested parties, and (3) a third arbitrator appointed by us.

The decisions of the court of arbitration shall become executory immediately and shall not be subject to appeal.

XIII. The Egyptian Government grants the concessionary company, for the entire life of the concession, the right to extract from mines and quarries belonging to the public domain, without payment of any fee, tax, or compensation, all materials necessary for the work of constructing and maintaining the installations and establishments belonging to the company.

Furthermore, it exempts the company from all customs, entry, and other duties on the importation into Egypt of all machinery and material of any kind that it may bring in from abroad for the needs of its various services during construction or operation.

XIV. We solemnly declare, for ourselves and our successors, subject to ratification by His Imperial Majesty the Sultan, that the great maritime canal from Suez to Pelusium and the ports belonging to it shall be open forever, as neutral passages, to every merchant vessel crossing from one sea to the other, without any distinction, exclusion, or preference with respect to persons or nationalities, in consideration of the payment of the fees, and compliance with the regulations established by the universal company, the concession-holder, for the use of the said canal and its appurtenances.

XV. In consequence of the principle laid down in the foregoing article, the universal company holding the concession may not, in any case, give to any vessel, company, or private party any advantage or favor not given to all other vessels, companies, or private parties on the same terms.

XVI. The life of the company is fixed at 99 years, counting from the completion of the work and the opening of the maritime canal to large vessels.

At the expiration of that period, the Egyptian Government will resume possession of the maritime canal constructed by the company, and it shall be its responsibility, in this case, to take over all materials and supplies used in the company's maritime service and, in return, to pay the company the value to be fixed, either by amicable agreement or on the basis of an opinion of experts.

Nevertheless, should the company retain the concession for successive periods of 99 years, the levy for the benefit of the Egyptian Government stipulated in Article XVIII below shall be increased for the second period to 20 percent, for the third period to 25 percent, and so on, at the rate of 5 percent for each period; but such levy shall, however, never exceed 35 percent of the net profits of the company.

XVII. In order to compensate the company for the expenses of construction, maintenance, and operation for which it is made responsible by these presents, we authorize it, henceforth and for its entire term of possession, as specified in paragraphs 1 and 3 of the foregoing article, to establish and collect, for passage in the canals and the ports belonging thereto, navigation, pilotage, towage, and anchorage fees, according to rate-schedules which it may change at any time, subject to the express condition that it shall: (1) Collect these fees without exception or favor from all vessels, under the same terms (2) Publish the rate-schedules three months before they become effective, in the capitals and principal commercial ports of the countries concerned (3) Not exceed for the special navigation fee the maximum figure of ten francs per ton of burden for vessels and ten francs a head for passengers.

The company may, also, for all water-supply facilities granted at the request of private parties, by virtue of Article VIII above, collect, according to rate-schedules which it will fix, a fee proportionate to the quantity of water used and the area of the land irrigated.

XVIII. At the same time, in view of the land grants and other advantages accorded the company in the foregoing articles, we shall make, for the benefit of the Egyptian Government, a levy of 15 percent of the net profits for each year as determined and apportioned at the general meeting of shareholders.

XIX. The list of charter members who contributed by their work, their studies, and their capital to the accomplishment of the undertaking, before the founding of the company, shall be prepared by us.

After deduction of the amount levied for the Egyptian Government stipulated in Article XVIII above, 10 percent of the annual net profits of the enterprise is to be allotted to the charter members or their heirs or assigns.

XX. Independently of the time necessary for the execution of the work, our friend and representative, Mr. Ferdinand de Lesseps, will preside over and direct the company as first founder for ten years from the time when the period of the enjoyment of the 99-year concession begins, under the terms of article XVI above.

XXI. The articles of incorporation of the company thus created under the name of Universal Company of the Maritime Canal of Suez are hereby approved; this approval constitutes authorization for establishment in the form of a corporation, effective on the date on which the capital of the company shall have been subscribed in full.

XXII. In token of the interest we attach to the success of the enterprise, we promise the company the loyal cooperation of the Egyptian Government and by these presents expressly request the officials and agents of all the departments of our Government to accord it assistance and protection under all circumstances.

Our engineers, Linant Bey and Mougel Bey, whom we place at the company's disposal for the direction and management of the work laid out by it, shall be in charge of the supervision of the workers and shall be responsible for enforcement of the regulations for putting the work programs into operation.

XXIII. All provisions of our ordonnance of November 30, 1854 are hereby revoked, together with any others which may be in conflict with the clauses

and terms of the present articles and conditions, which alone shall govern the concession to which they apply.
Done at Alexandria, January 5, 1856.

To my loyal friend of high birth and high rank, Mr. Ferdinand de Lesseps:
Since the concession granted to the Universal Company of the Canal of Suez must be approved by His Imperial Majesty the Sultan, I am transmitting to you this authentic copy so that you may establish the said financial company.
As for the work connected with cutting through the Isthmus, the company may carry it out itself as soon as the authorization of the Sublime Porte is granted to me.
Alexandria, Rebi-ul-Akher 26, 1272 (January 5, 1856).
O. Seal of His Highness the Viceroy.

APPENDIX B

Convention Between Great Britain, Austria–Hungary, France, Germany, Italy, the Netherlands, Russia, Spain, and Turkey, Respecting the Free Navigation of the Suez Maritime Canal. Constantinople, October 29, 1888.*

In the name of Almighty God,

Her Majesty the Queen of the United Kingdom of Great Britain and Ireland, Empress of India; His Majesty the German Emperor, King of Prussia; His Majesty the Emperor of Austia, King of Bohemia, etc., and Apostolic King of Hungary; His Majesty the King of Spain, and in His Name the Queen Regent of the Kingdom; the President of the French Republic; His Majesty the King of Italy; His Majesty the King of the Netherlands, Grand Duke of Luxemburg, etc.; His Majesty the Emperor of all the Russias; and His Majesty the Emperor of the Ottomans, being desirous of establishing, by a Conventional Act, a definitive system intended to guarantee, at all times and to all the Powers, the free use of the Suez Maritime Canal, and thus to complete the system under which the navigation of this canal has been placed by the Firman of His Imperial Majesty the Sultan, dated February 22, 1866 (2 Zilkadé, 1282), and sanctioning the Concessions of His Highness the Khedive, have appointed as their plenipotentiaries, to wit:

Her Majesty the Queen of the United Kingdom of Great Britain and Ireland, Empress of India, the Right Honorable Sir William Arthur White, Her Ambassador Extraordinary and Plenipotentiary;

His Majesty the German Emperor, King of Prussia, His Excellency Joseph de Radowitz, His Ambassador Extraordinary and Plenipotentiary;

His Majesty the Emperor of Austria, King of Bohemia, etc., and Apostolic King of Hungary, His Excellency Baron Henri de Calice, His Ambassador Extraordinary and Plenipotentiary;

His Majesty the King of Spain and in His Name the Queen Regent of the Kingdom, Mr. Miguel Florez y Garcia, His Chargé d'Affaires;

The President of the French Republic, His Excellency Gustave Louis Lannes, Count de Montebello, Ambassador Extraordinary and Plenipotentiary of France;

His Majesty the King of Italy, His Excellency Baron Albert Blanc, His Ambassador Extraordinary and Plenipotentiary;

His Majesty the King of the Netherlands, Grand Duke of Luxemburg, etc., Mr. Gustave Keun, His Chargé d'Affaires;

His Majesty the Emperor of all the Russias, His Excellency Alexandre de Nélidow, His Ambassador Extraordinary and Plenipotentiary;

* English translation from United States Department of State, *The Suez Canal Problem*, pp. 16–20.

His Majesty the Emperor of the Ottomans, Mehemmed Said Pasha, His Minister of Foreign Affairs;

Who, having communicated to each other their respective full powers, found in good and due form, have agreed upon the following articles:

Art. I. The Suez Maritime Canal shall always be free and open, in time of war as in time of peace, to every vessel of commerce or of war, without distinction of flag.

Consequently, the High Contracting Parties agree not in any way to interfere with the free use of the Canal, in time of war as in time of peace.

The Canal shall never be subject to the exercise of the right of blockade.

Art. II. The High Contracting Parties, recognizing that the Fresh-Water Canal is indispensable to the Maritime Canal, take cognizance of the engagements of His Highness the Khedive towards the Universal Suez Canal Company as regards the Fresh-Water Canal; which engagements are stipulated in a Convention dated March 18, 1863, containing a preamble and four Articles.

They undertake not to interfere in any way with the security of that Canal and its branches, the working of which shall not be the object of any attempt at obstruction.

Art. III. The High Contracting Parties likewise undertake to respect the equipment, establishments, buildings and work of the Maritime Canal and of the Fresh-Water Canal.

Art. IV. The Maritime Canal remaining open in time of war as a free passage, even to ships of war of the belligerents, under the terms of Article I of the present Treaty, the High Contracting Parties agree that no right of war, act of hostility or act having for its purpose to interfere with the free navigation of the Canal, shall be committed in the Canal and its ports of access, or within a radius of 3 nautical miles from those ports, even though the Ottoman Empire should be one of the belligerent Powers.

Warships of belligerents shall not take on fresh supplies or lay in stores in the Canal and its ports of access, except in so far as may be strictly necessary. The transit of the said vessels through the Canal shall be effected as quickly as possible, in accordance with the regulations in force, and without stopping except for the necessities of the service.

Their stay at Port Said and the roadstead of Suez shall not exceed 24 hours, except in case of putting in through stress of weather. In such case, they shall be bound to depart as soon as possible. A period of 24 hours shall always elapse between the sailing of a belligerent ship from a port of access and the departure of a ship belonging to the enemy Power.

Art. V. In time of war, belligerent powers shall not discharge or take on troops, munitions, or war materiel in the Canal and its ports of access. In case of an accidental hindrance in the Canal, however, troops broken up into groups not exceeding 1000 men, with a corresponding amount of equipment, may be embarked or disembarked at the ports of access.

Art. VI. Prizes shall in all respects be subject to the same rules and regulations as the warships of belligerents.

Art. VII. The Powers shall not keep any warship in the waters of the Canal (including Lake Timsah and the Bitter Lakes).

They may, however, have warships, the number of which shall not exceed two for each Power, stationed in the ports of access of Port Said and Suez.

This right shall not be exercised by belligerents.

Art. VIII. The Agents in Egypt of the Signatory Powers of the present Treaty shall be charged to see that it is carried out. In any circumstance threatening the security and free passage of the Canal, they shall meet at the summons of three of them and under the presidency of their Doyen, to the necessary verifications. They shall inform the Khedivial Government of the danger perceived, in order that it may take proper steps to assure the protection and the free use of the Canal. In any case, they shall meet once a year to take note of the due execution of the Treaty.

These latter meetings shall be presided over by a Special Commissioner appointed for that purpose by the Imperial Ottoman Government. A Khedivial Commissioner may also take part in the meeting, and may preside over it in case of the absence of the Ottoman Commissioner.

They shall demand, in particular, the removal of any work or the dispersion of any assemblage on either bank of the Canal, the purpose or effect of which might be to interfere with the freedom and complete safety of navigation.

Art. IX. The Egyptian Government shall, within the limits of its powers based on the Firmans, and under the conditions provided for in the present Treaty, take the necessary measures for enforcing the execution of the said Treaty.

In case the Egyptian Government should not have sufficient means at its disposal, it shall appeal to the Imperial Ottoman Government which shall take the necessary measures for responding to such appeal, give notice thereof to the other Signatory Powers of the Declaration of London of March 17, 1885, and, if necessary, consult with them on the matter.

The provisions of Articles IV, V, VI, and VII shall not stand in the way of the measures taken by virtue of the present Article.

Art. X. Likewise, the provisions of Articles IV, V, VII, and VIII shall not stand in the way of any measures which His Majesty the Sultan and His Highness the Khedive in the name of His Imperial Majesty, and within the limits of the Firmans granted, might find it necessary to take to assure by their own forces the defense of Egypt and the maintenance of public order.

In case His Imperial Majesty the Sultan or His Highness the Khedive should find it necessary to avail himself of the exceptions provided for in the present Article, the Signatory Powers of the Declaration of London would be notified thereof by the Imperial Ottoman Government.

It is also understood that the provisions of the four Articles in question shall in no case stand in the way of measures which the Imperial Ottoman Government considers it necessary to take to assure by its own forces the defense of its other possessions situated on the eastern coast of the Red Sea.

Art. XI. The measures taken in the cases provided for by Articles IX and X of the present Treaty shall not interfere with the free use of the Canal. In the same cases, the erection of permanent fortifications contrary to the provisions of Article VIII is prohibited.

Art. XII. The High Contracting Parties, by application of the principle of equality as regards free use of the Canal, a principle which forms one of the bases of the present Treaty, agree that none of them shall seek, with respect to the Canal, territorial or commercial advantages or privileges in any international arrangements that may be concluded. Furthermore, the rights of Turkey as the territorial Power are reserved.

Art. XIII. Aside from the obligations expressly provided for by the clauses of the present Treaty, the sovereign rights of His Imperial Majesty the Sultan and the rights and immunities of His Highness the Khedive based on the Firmans are in no way affected.

Art. XIV. The High Contracting Parties agree that the engagements resulting from the present Treaty shall not be limited by the duration of the Acts of Concession of the Universal Suez Canal Company.

Art. XV. The stipulations of the present Treaty shall not interfere with the sanitary measures in force in Egypt.

Art. XVI. The High Contracting Parties undertake to bring the present Treaty to the knowledge of those States which have not signed it, inviting them to accede thereto.

Art. XVII. The present Treaty shall be ratified, and the ratifications thereof shall be exchanged at Constantinople within one month or sooner if possible.

In witness whereof the respective Plenipotentiaries have signed the present Treaty, and have affixed thereto the seal of their arms.

Done at Constantinople, on the 29th day of the month of October, of the year 1888.

For Great Britain	(L. S.) W. A. White
Germany	(L. S.) Radowitz
Austria-Hungary	(L. S.) Calice
Spain	(L. S.) Miguel Florez y Garcia
France	(L. S.) G. De Montebello
Italy	(L. S.) A. Blanc
Netherlands	(L. S.) Gus. Keun
Russia	(L. S.) Nélidow
Turkey	(L. S.) M. Said

APPENDIX C

Situation Created by the Unilateral Action of the Egyptian Government in Bringing to an End the System of International Operation of the Suez Canal, which was Confirmed and Completed by the Suez Canal Convention of 1888.

RESOLUTION
ADOPTED BY THE SECURITY COUNCIL
AT ITS 743RD MEETING ON 13 OCTOBER 1956*

The Security Council

Noting the declarations made before it and the accounts of the development of the exploratory conversations on the Suez question given by the Secretary-General of the United Nations and the Foreign Minister of Egypt, France and the United Kingdom;

Agrees that any settlement of the Suez question should meet the following requirements:

1. There should be free and open transit through the Canal without discrimination, overt or covert - this covers both political and technical aspects;
2. The sovereignty of Egypt should be respected;
3. The operation of the Canal should be insulated from the politics of any country;
4. The manner of fixing tolls and charges should be decided by agreement between Egypt and the users;
5. A fair proportion of the dues should be allotted to development;
6. In case of disputes, unresolved affairs between the Suez Canal Company and the Egyptian Government should be settled by arbitration with suitable terms of reference and suitable provisions for the payment of sums found to be due.

---

* U.N. Sec. Council, Doc. S/3675.

APPENDIX D

Declaration on the Suez Canal and the Arrangements for its Operation.

LETTER
DATED 24 APRIL 1957
FROM THE MINISTER FOR FOREIGN AFFAIRS OF EGYPT
ADDRESSED TO THE SECRETARY–GENERAL*

The Government of Egypt are pleased to announce that the Suez Canal is now open for normal traffic and will thus once again serve as a link between the nations of the world in the cause of peace and prosperity.

The Government of Egypt wish to acknowledge with appreciation and gratitude the efforts of the States and peoples of the world who contributed to the restoration of the Canal for normal traffic, and of the United Nations whose exertions made it possible that the clearance of the Canal be accomplished peacefully and in a short time.

On 18 March 1957, the Government of Egypt set forth in a memorandum basic principles relating to the Suez Canal and the arrangements for its operation. The memorandum contemplated a further detailed statement on the subject. In pursuance of the above, I have the honour to enclose a copy of the declaration made today by the Government of Egypt in fulfillment of their participation in the Constantinople Convention of 1888, noting their understanding of the Security Council resolution of 13 October 1956 and in line with their statements relating to it before the Council.

I have the honour to invite Your Excellency's attention to the last paragraph of the declaration which provides that it will be deposited and registered with the Secretariat of the United Nations. The declaration, with the obligations therein, constitutes an international instrument and the Government of Egypt request that you kindly receive and register it accordingly.

MAHMOUD FAWZI
Minister of Foreign Affairs of Egypt.

Declaration

In elaboration of the principles set forth in their memorandum dated 18 March 1957, the Government of the Republic of Egypt, in accord with the Constantinople Convention of 1888 and the Charter of the United Nations,

* U.N. Sec. Council, Doc. S/3818.

make hereby the following Declaration on the Suez Canal and the arrangements for its operation.

1. *Reaffirmation of Convention*

It remains the unaltered policy and firm purpose of the Government of Egypt to respect the terms and the spirit of the Constantinople Convention of 1888 and the rights and obligations arising therefrom. The Government of Egypt will continue to respect, observe and implement them.

2. *Observance of the Convention and of the Charter of the United Nations*

While reaffirming their determination to respect the terms and the spirit of the Constantinople Convention of 1888 and to abide by the Charter and the principles and purposes of the United Nations, the Government of Egypt are confident that the other signatories of the said Convention and all others concerned will be guided by the same resolve.

3. *Freedom of navigation, tolls, and development of the Canal*

The Government of Egypt are more particularly determined:

(a) To afford and maintain free and uninterrupted navigation for all nations within the limits of and in accordance with the provisions of the Constantinople Convention of 1888;

(b) That tolls shall continue to be levied in accordance with the last agreement, concluded on 28 April 1936, between the Government of Egypt and the Suez Canal Maritime Company, and that any increase in the current rate of tolls within any twelve months, if it takes place, shall be limited to 1 per cent, any increase beyond that level to be the result of negotiations, and, failing agreement, be settled by arbitration according to the procedure set forth in paragraph 7 (b).

(c) That the Canal is maintained and developed in accordance with the progressive requirements of modern navigation and that such maintenance and development shall include the 8th and 9th Programmes of the Suez Canal Maritime Company with such improvements to them as are considered necessary.

4. *Operation and management*

The Canal will be operated and managed by the autonomous Suez Canal Authority established by the Government of Egypt on 26 July 1956. The Government of Egypt are looking forward with confidence to continued co-operation with the nations of the world in advancing the usefulness of the Canal. To that end the Government of Egypt would welcome and encourage co-operation between the Suez Canal Authority and representatives of shipping and trade.

5. *Financial Arrangements*

(a) Tolls shall be payable in advance to the account of the Suez Canal Authority at any bank as may be authorized by it. In pursuance of this, the Suez Canal Authority has authorized the National Bank of Egypt and is negotiating with the Bank for International Settlements to accept on its behalf payment of the Canal tolls.

(b) The Suez Canal Authority shall pay to the Government of Egypt 5 per cent of all the gross receipts as royalty.

(c) The Suez Canal Authority will establish a Suez Canal Capital and Development Fund into which shall be paid 25 per cent of all gross receipts. This Fund will assure that there shall be available to the Suez Canal Authority adequate resources to meet the needs of development and capital expenditure for the fulfilment of the responsibilities they have assumed and are fully determined to discharge.

6. *Canal Code*

The regulations governing the Canal, including the details of its operation, are embodied in the Canal Code which is the law of the Canal. Due notice will be given of any alteration in the Code, and any such alteration, if it affects the principles and commitments in this Declaration and is challenged or complained against for that reason, shall be dealt with in accordance with the procedure set forth in paragraph 7 (b).

7. *Discrimination and complaints relating to the Canal Code*

(a) In pursuance of the principles laid down in the Constantinople Convention of 1888, the Suez Canal Authority, by the terms of its Charter, can in no case grant any vessel, company or other party any advantage or favour not accorded to other vessels, companies or parties on the same conditions.

(b) Complaints of discrimination or violation of the Canal Code shall be sought to be resolved by the complaining party by reference to the Suez Canal Authority. In the event that such a reference does not resolve the complaint, the matter may be referred, at the option of the complaining party or the Authority, to an arbitration tribunal composed of one nominee of the complaining party, one of the Authority and a third to be chosen by both. In case of disagreement, such third member will be chosen by the President of the International Court of Justice upon the application of either party.

(c) The decisions of the arbitration tribunal shall be made by a majority of its members. The decisions shall be binding upon the parties when they are rendered and they must be carried out in good faith.

(d) The Government of Egypt will study further appropriate arrangements that could be made for fact-finding, consultation and arbitration on complaints relating to the Canal Code.

8. *Compensation and claims*

The question of compensation and claims in connexion with the nationalization of the Suez Canal Maritime Company shall, unless agreed between the parties concerned, be referred to arbitration in accordance with the established international practice.

9. *Disputes, disagreements or differences arising out of the Convention and
   this Declaration.*

(a) Disputes or disagreements arising in respect of the Constantinople Convention of 1888 or this Declaration shall be settled in accordance with the Charter of the United Nations.

(b) Differences arising between the parties to the said Convention in respect of the interpretation or the applicability of its provisions, if not otherwise resolved, will be referred to the International Court of Justice. The Government of Egypt would take the necessary steps in order to accept the compulsory jurisdiction of the International Court of Justice in conformity with the provisions of Article 36 of its Statute.

10. *Status of this Declaration*

The Government of Egypt make this Declaration, which re-affirms and is in full accord with the terms and spirit of the Constantinople Convention of 1888, as an expression of their desire and determination to enable the Suez Canal to be an efficient and adequate waterway linking the nations of the world and serving the cause of peace and prosperity.

This Declaration, with the obligations therein, constitutes an international instrument and will be deposited and registered with the Secretariat of the United Nations.

LETTER
DATED 18 JULY 1957
FROM THE MINISTER FOR FOREIGN AFFAIRS
OF EGYPT ADDRESSED TO THE SECRETARY-GENERAL
*relating to paragraph 9 (b) of the Declaration**

Declaration

I, Mahmoud Fawzi, Minister for Foreign Affairs of the Republic of Egypt, declare on behalf of the Government of the Republic of Egypt, that, in accordance with art. 36 (2) of the Statute of the International Court of Justice and in pursuance and for the purposes of paragraph 9 (b) of the declaration of the Government of the Republic of Egypt dated 24 April 1957 on "the Suez Canal and the arrangements for its operation," the Government of the Republic of Egypt accept as compulsory *ipso facto*, on condition of reciprocity and without special agreement, the jurisdiction of the International Court of Justice in all legal disputes that may arise under the said paragraph 9 (b) of the above declaration dated 24 April 1957, with effect as from that date.

* U.N. Sec. Council, Doc. S/3818/Add. 1.

BIBLIOGRAPHY

A. History Of The Suez Canal

Aglietti, B., *Il Canale di Suez ed i Rapporti Anglo–Egiziani*, (Biblioteca di Studi Coloniali, IX), Firenze, 1939.

Charles–Roux, J., *L'Isthme et le Canal de Suez. Historique – Etat Actuel*, 2 vols., Paris, 1901.

Connell, J., *The Most Important Country. The true story of the Suez Crisis and the events leading to it*, London, 1957.

Crabitès, P., *The Spoliation of Suez*, London, 1940.

Dewhurst, C., *Limelight for Suez*, Cairo, 1946.

Egyptian Government, *Journal Officiel*.

France, Ministère des Affaires Etrangères, *Documents Diplomatiques*.

Great Britain, *Parliamentary Papers*.

—   , *Command Papers*.

Hallberg, C. W., *The Suez Canal. Its History and Diplomatic Importance*, New York, 1931.

Hoskins, H. L., *The Middle East. Problem Area in World Politics*, New York, 1954.

Johnson, P., *The Suez War*, London, 1957.

Lavergne, B., *Problemes Africains. – Afrique Noire – Algérie – Affaire de Suez*, Paris, 1957.

Lesseps, F. de, *Percement de l'Isthme de Suez, Exposé et Documents officiels*, Paris, 1855.

—   , *Lettres, Journal et Documents pour servir à l'Histoire du Canal de Suez*, 5 vols., Paris, 1875–81.

—   , *Origines du Canal de Suez*, Paris (n. d.).

Longgood, W. F., *Suez Story. Key to the Middle East*, New York, 1957.

Marlowe, J., *Anglo-Egyptian Relations. 1800–1953*, London, 1954.

Moussa, F., *Les Négociations Anglo-Egyptiennes de 1950–1951 sur Suez et le Soudan. Essai de Critique Historique*, Genève, 1955.

Nasser, G. A., *Egypt's Liberation. The Philosophy of the Revolution*, Washington, 1955.

Nutting, A., *I Saw for Myself. The Aftermath of Suez*. London, 1958.

Rammontel, P., *Le Canal de Suez, grande oeuvre française*, Paris, 1954.

Reymond, P., *Histoire de la Navigation dans le Canal de Suez*, Le Caire, 1956.

Royal Institute of International Affairs, *The Middle East, A Political and Economic Survey*, 2nd ed., London, 1954.

Sammarco, A., *Suez. Storia e Problemi secondo documenti inediti egiziani ed europei*, Milano, 1943.

Schonfield, H. J., *The Suez Canal in World Affairs*. London, 1952.

Siegfried, A., *Suez, Panama et les Routes Maritimes Mondiales*, Paris, 1940.

United States, Department of State, *The Suez Canal Problem, July 26–September 22, 1956. A Documentary Publication*, Dept. of State Publication 6392.

—   *United States Policy in the Middle East. September 1956–June 1957. Documents*, Dept. of State publication 6505.

Watt, D. C., *Britain and the Suez Canal*, London, 1956.

Wilson, Sir A. T., *The Suez Canal. Its Past, Present and Future*, London, 1933.

B. LEGAL PROBLEMS CONCERNING THE SUEZ CANAL

Accioly, H., *Tratado de Direito Internacional Público*, 2nd ed., 3 vols., Rio de Janeiro, 1956.
Allen, H. C., *Great Britain and the United States. A History of Anglo-American Relations, 1783–1952*, New York, 1955.
Ambrosini, G., *La Situazione Internazionale dell'Egitto e il Regime del Canale di Suez, (Rivista di Studi Politici Internazionali*, 4 (1937) N.1).
Asser, M. T., *La Convention de Constantinople pour le libre usage du Canal de Suez, (Revue de Droit International et de Législation Comparée*, 20 (1888) 529–558).
Avram, B., *The Evolution of the Suez Canal Status from 1869 up to 1956. A Historico-Juridical Study*, (Thèse), Genève, 1958.
Badawi, A. H., *Le Statut International du Canal de Suez. Aperçu historique*, in *Grundprobleme des Internationalen Rechts. Festschrift für Jean Spiropoulos*, Bonn, 1957, pp. 13–33.
Badeau, J. S., *The Significance of the Suez Canal in Current International Affairs.* Near East Society, Monograph Series, No. 16.
Bahon, M., *Le libre usage du Canal de Suez et sa "Neutralité,"* Académie de Marine (Séance du 23 Avril 1936).
Benno, I., J., *La situation internationale du Canal de Suez*, (Thèse), Lyon, 1929.
Berkol, F. N., *Le Statut Juridique actuel des Portes Maritimes Orientales de la Méditerranée* (Les Détroits–Le Canal de Suez), (Thèse), Paris, 1940.
Biscottini, G., *Contributo alla Teoria degli Atti Unilaterali nel Diritto Internazionale*, Milano, 1951.
Bluntschli, *Le Droit International Codifié.* Traduit de l'allemand par M. C. Lardy, 5th ed., Paris, 1895.
Bourquin, M., *L'Organisation internationale des Voies de Communication*, (*Recueil des Cours*, 1924, IV, 163–210).
Brüel, E., *International Straits. A Treatise on International Law*, 2 vols., Copenhagen and London, 1947.
Buell, R. L., *The Suez Canal and League Sanctions*, (*Geneva Special Studies*, 6 (1935) No. 3).
Calvo, C., *Le Droit International Théorique et Pratique*, 5th ed., 6 vols., Paris, 1896.
Camand, M. L., *Etude sur le Régime Juridique du Canal de Suez*, (Thèse), Grenoble, 1899.
Cansacchi, G., *La Notificazione Internazionale*, Istituto per gli Studi di Politica Internazionale, (n. d.).
Cavaglieri, A., *Règles Générales du Droit de la Paix*, (*Recueil des Cours*, 1929, I, 315–585).
Contuzzi, F. P., *La Neutralizzazione del Canale di Suez e la Diplomazia Europea*, Firenze, 1888.
Decleva, M., *Gli Accordi Taciti Internazionali*, Padova, 1957.
Dedreux, R., *Der Suezkanal im internationalen Rechte unter Berücksichtigung seiner Vorgeschichte*, Tübingen, 1913.
Diena, G., *Il Canale di Suez ed il Patto de la Società delle Nazioni*, (Atti del Reale Istituto Veneto di Scienze, Lettere ed Arti, 96, 2nd Part (1936–37) 323–333).
Dupuis, C., *Liberté des Voies de communication. Relations Internationales*, (*Recueil des Cours*, 1924, I, 129–444).
El-Hefnaoui, M., *Les Problèmes Contemporaines posés par le Canal de Suez*, (Thèse), Paris, 1951.
Fauchille, P., *Etude sur le Blocus Maritime*, Paris, 1882.
—— , *Traité de Droit International Public*, 8me ed., 2 vols., Paris 1921–1926.
Foighel, I., *Nationalization. A Study in the Protection of Alien Property in International Law*, Copenhagen, 1957.
Fournier de Flaix, E., *L'Indépendance de l'Egypte et le Régime International du Canal de Suez*, Paris, 1883.
Garner, J. W., *The International Binding Force of Unilateral Oral Declarations*, (*American Journal of International Law*, 27 (1933) 493–497).
Guggenheim, P., *Traité de Droit international public. Avec mention de la pratique internationale et suisse*, 2 vols., Genève, 1953.

Guibal, R., *Peut-on fermer le Canal de Suez?*, Paris, 1937.
Guillien, R., *Un cas de dédoublement fonctionnel et de législation de fait internationale: Le statut du Canal de Suez*, in "*La Technique et les Principes du Droit Public. Etudes en l'honneur de Georges Scelle*," Paris, 1950, v. 2, pp. 735–752.
Hains, P. C., *Neutralization of the Panama Canal*, (*American Journal of International Law*, 3 (1909) 354–394).
Hershey, A. S., *The International Law and Diplomacy of the Russo-Japanese War*, London, 1906.
Higgins and Colombos, *The International Law of the Sea*, 2nd ed., London, 1951.
Holland, T. E., *The International Position of the Suez Canal*, in *Studies in International Law*, Oxford, 1898, ch. 14.
Hoskins, H. L., *The Suez Canal in Time of War*, (*Foreign Affairs*, 14 (1935–1936) 93–101).
— , *The Suez Canal as an International Waterway*, (*American Journal of International Law*. 37 (1943) 373–385).
Hostie, J., *Examen de quelques Règles du Droit International dans le domaine des Communications et du Transit*, (*Recueil des Cours*, 1932, II, 403–524).
Husny, H., *Le Canal de Suez et la Politique Egyptienne*, (Thèse), Montpellier, 1923.
Institut de Droit International, *Conditions de neutralisation ou de protection internationale du Canal de Suez*, Annuaire, Troisième et Quatrième Années, t.1, pp. 111–128 and 328–350.
Inter-Parliamentary Union, *Resolutions adopted by Inter-Parliamentary Conferences and Principal Decisions of the Council, 1911–1936*, Geneva, 1937.
Istituto per Gli Studi di Politica Internazionale, *Il Canale di Suez, nella Storia, nell' Economia, nel Diritto*, Milano, 1935.
Jiménez de Aréchaga, E., *Treaty Stipulations in favor of Third States*, (*American Journal of International Law*, 50 (1956) 338–357).
Knapp, H. S., *The Real Status of the Panama Canal as regards Neutralization*, (*American Journal of International Law*, 4 (1910) 314–358).
Lawrence, T. J., *The Suez Canal in International Law*, in *Essays on Some Disputed Questions in Modern International Law*, Cambridge, 1885, 2nd ed., Essay II.
Le Fur, L., *Espagne et Etats-Unis. Guerre. Conduite du Conflit: rapports entre les belligérants et les neutres*, (*Revue Générale de Droit International Public*, 6 (1899) 196–229).
McNair, A., *The Functions and differing legal character of Treaties*, (*British Yearbook of International Law*, 11 (1930) 100–118).
Metternich, Prince de, *Mémoires, Documents et Ecrits Divers laissés par le Prince de...*, 8 vols., Paris, 1880–84.
Molfino, G., *Il Canale di Suez e il suo regime internazionale*, Genova, 1936.
Moussa, A., *Essai sur le Canal de Suez. Droit et Politique*, (Thèse), Paris, 1935.
Oppenheim, L., *The Panama Canal Conflict between Great Britain and The United States of America*, Cambridge, 1913.
Oppenheim–Lauterpacht, *International Law. A Treatise*, 2 vols., v. I (8th ed.,), v. II (7th ed.,), London, 1952–1955.
Poiaga, A., *Suez. Aspetti del Problema: Cenni Storici*, Milano, 1939.
Pradier–Fodéré, P., *Traité de Droit International Public Européen et Americain*, 8 vols., Paris, 1885–1906.
Prize Cases heard and decided in the Prize Court during the Great War by the R. H. Sir Samuel Evans, and in the Courts of the Overseas Dominions and on Appeal to the Judicial Committee of the Privy Council, 3 vols., London, 1916–1922.
Quintano Ripollés, A., *El Canal de Suez*, Madrid, 1953.
Root, E., *Addresses on International Subjects*, Cambridge, 1916.
Rossignol, L. M., *Le Canal de Suez. Etude Historique, Juridique et Politique*, Paris, 1898.
Rousseau, C., *L'application des sanctions contre l'Italie et le Droit International*, (*Revue de Droit International et de Legislation Comparée*, 3rd ser., 17 (1936) 5–64).
— , *Droit International Public*, Paris, 1953.
Roxburgh, R. F., *International Conventions and Third States*, London, 1917.
Saint Victor, G., *Le Canal de Suez*, Paris, 1934.

Scelle, G., *La Nationalisation du Canal de Suez et le Droit International,* (*Annuaire Français de Droit International,* 2 (1956) 3–19).

Schiarabati, A., *De la condition juridique du Canal de Suez avant et après la Grande Guerre,* (Thèse), Lyon, 1930.

Sibert, M., *Traité de Droit International Public,* 2 vols., Paris, 1951.

Society of Comparative Legislation, *The Suez Canal. A Selection of Documents relating to the International Status of the Suez Canal and the position of the Suez Canal Company,* London, 1956.

Sottile, A., *Méditerranée, Suez et Liberté de navigation,* (*Revue de Droit International, de Sciences Diplomatiques et Politiques,* 18 (1940) 123–132).

Suez Canal Company, *The Suez Canal Company and the Decision taken by the Egyptian Government on 26th July 1956,* Paris, 1956.

Twiss, T., *On International Conventions for the Neutralization of Territory and their application to the Suez Canal,* London, 1887.

Vali, F. A., *Servitudes of International Law. A Study of Rights in Foreign Territory,* 2nd ed., London, 1958.

Verdross, A., *Le Droit International de la Paix,* (*Recueil des Cours,* 1929, V, 275–517).

— , *Derecho Internacional Público,* Trad. castellana, Madrid, 1955.

Visscher, P., *Les Aspects Juridiques Fondamentaux de la Question de Suez,* (*Revue Générale de Droit International Public,* 3me sér., 29 (1958) 400–443).

Whittuck, E. A., *International Canals.* (Peace Handbooks, v. 23, No. 150), London, 1920.

Wilson, A., *Some International and Legal Aspects of the Suez Canal,* (*Transactions of the Grotius Society* 21 (1935) 127–147).

Yeghen, F., *Le Canal de Suez et la Réglementation internationale des Canaux inter-oceaniques,* (Thèse), Dijon, 1927.

INDEX

Aaland Islands Question: 33.
Abbas Hilmi, Khedive of Egypt: 13.
Abbas Pasha, Viceroy of Egypt: 5, 6.
Aben-Jafas-Al-Mansour, Second Abbasid Caliph: 4.
Abuse of rights: 37, 38, 39.
Agreement of April 8, 1904: See Anglo-French Agreement of.
Anglo-French Agreement of April 8, 1904: 12, 13.
  and Constantinople Convention of 1888: 70, 71.
Anzilotti, Judge: 36, 44, 88.
Arabi, Colonel: 9, 10, 56, 62, 63, 67.
Armistice Agreement of Feb. 1949: 85, 86, 105.
Association of Chambers of Commerce of Great Britain: 61.
Aswan Dam: 18.
Azevedo, Judge: 24.

Bank for International Settlements: 93.
Black Saturday: 17.
British Notification of Oct. 23, 1914: 81.
British occupation of Egypt: 10, 12, 13, 14, 15, 63, 82, 103.
British Prize Court for Egypt: 48, 59, 60, 80, 81, 82.

Circular Letter of Jan. 1, 1873: 55.
Circular Letter of May 1918: 81.
Compagnie Universelle du Canal Maritime de Suez: see Suez Canal Co.
Concadoro Case: 80, 82.
Concession of November 30, 1854:
  Art. 4 of: 62.
  Art. 6 of: 50, 57.
  Art. 10 of: 95.
  communicated to the Powers: 50.
  effects on sovereignty: 94.
  effects on the Suez Canal Company: 96.
  origin of: 2, 5.
Concession of Jan. 5, 1856:
  origin of: 2, 5.
  summary of: 5–6.
  ratification of: 6.
  Art. 14 of: 51, 54, 57, 60, 62, 73, 97, 99, 101.
  Art. 16 of: 95.
  Art. 17 of: 96, 104.
  interpretation of: 92.

legal character of: 60.
  effects on sovereignty: 94.
  effects on the Suez Canal Co.: 91, 98.
  and Constantinople Convention of 1888: 100.
  text of: 114–118.
Condominium over the Sudan: 13.
Conference of Barcelona of 1921: 1, 23, 44, 45.
Conference of Constantinople of 1873: 55, 56, 58, 61, 98.
Conference of Constantinople of 1882: 9, 62.
Conference of London of Aug. 1956: 18, 19, 91, 93, 100, 107.
Conference of London of Sept. 1956: 19, 107.
Conference of Paris of 1885:
  origin of: 11, 64.
  discussion of the delegates at: 59, 64, 65, 99.
  British reservation at: 70.
  and violations of the freedom of navigation in the Suez Canal: 72.
Conference on the Law of the Sea of 1958: 24.
Congress of Paris of 1856: 22, 23, 62.
Congress of Vienna of 1815: 22, 23.
Convention and Statute on the Regime of Navigable Waterways. See Conference of Barcelona.
Convention of Constantinople of 1888: 1, 2, 3.
  conclusion of: 11.
  British reservation to: 70, 71.
  guaranty of: 67.
  freedom of navigation clauses of: 48, 66, 67, 69, 70.
  neutrality clauses of: 67, 68, 69.
  demilitarization and internationalization clauses of: 69.
  legal effects of: on Ottoman Empire, 71–72; on Egypt, 71, 72, 73, 74, 75, 87, 88, 89; on the international community, 72, 73; on signatory States, 73; on successor States, 73, 74, 75; on non-signatory States, 30, 75, 76, 77, 78, 87, 88, 104.
  and the Concessions: 99, 100, 101, 102.
  and regime of internationality: 97, 101, 104.

and British occupation of Egypt: 54.
and Draft Treaty of Paris of 1885: 64, 65.
and the practice of States: 78–88.
and Egyptian Declaration of 1957: 108, 111.
revision of: 112.
text of: 119–122.
Convention of Feb. 22, 1866: 7, 53, 57, 62, 92, 94, 100.
Convention on the Territorial Sea: 24.
Corfu Channel Case: 24, 41.
Corinth Canal: 1.
Court of Appeal of Paris: 91.
Credit Alexandrin v. Cie. Universelle du Canal Maritime de Suez Case: 92, 93.
Curzon, Lord: 70.
Custom:
    and stipulations in favour of third States: 34, 35.
    and the Constantinople Convention of 1888: 78, 80, 86, 87.
Customs Regime between Germany and Austria Case: 27.

Declaration Concerning Egypt and Morocco: 12.
Declaration of April 24, 1957: 20, 108, 109, 110, 111, 124.
Declaration of independence of Egypt: 14, 15, 16, 74, 82, 83, 92, 103.
Declaration of London of March 17, 1885: 11, 64, 69, 83.
Declaration regarding the Suez Canal: 74.
Derflinger Case: 82.
Disraeli, Benjamin: 8, 91, 99.
Dulles, John Foster: 91.

Eastern Greenland Case: 27.
Egypt v. The British India Navigation Co. Case: 44.
Egyptian Declaration of April 24, 1957: 20, 108–111, 124.
Egyptian Military Proclamation of Sept. 4, 1939: 83.
Egyptian Nationalism: 9, 13, 14, 16, 17.
Egyptian Note of Dec. 20, 1945: 16, 17.
Egyptian Note of May 28, 1947: 84, 86, 87.
Egyptian Prize Court of Alexandria: 85.
Egyptian Proclamation of May 15, 1948: 85.
Egyptian Revolution of 1952: 17, 18.
Ethiopian War of 1935. See Italo-Abyssinian War of 1935.

Farouk, King: 16, 17.
Firman of June 1841: 5.

Firman of March 19, 1866: 7, 53, 54, 62, 63, 92.
Five-Power Proposal: 19.
Flying Trader Case: 85.
Franco-German War of 1870: 58, 63.
Free Zones of Upper Savoy and the District of Gex Case: 30, 31, 33.
Freedom of the Seas: 37, 38, 41, 42.

German Proclamation of Nov. 14, 1936: 36, 37.
German Supreme Court (British Zone):
    and international canals: 26, 42, 43.
    and Kiel Canal: 37.
Gladstone, Lord: 56.
Grand Vizier of Turkey: 51.
Granville, Lord: 10, 63.
Gutenfels Case: 48, 59, 60, 80, 82.

Hitler, Chancellor: 36.
Hopkins, Harry L.: 84.
Hoskins, Admiral: 9, 63.
Huber, Judge: 36, 44, 88.
Hussein Kamel Pasha, Prince: 13.

Institut de Droit International: 1.
International Authority for the Suez Canal: 107.
International Canals:
    definition: 24, 25, 26, 48.
    sovereign's consent required: 26, 27.
    consent given by a unilateral declaration: 28–29.
    consent given in a multilateral treaty: 29–35.
    consent given tacitly: 35, 36.
    consent given in a treaty of peace: 36, 37.
    and freedom of the seas: 37, 38.
    and the principle of international public utility: 38.
    and abuse of rights: 38, 39.
    summary of doctrine on: 39.
    relation to international rivers and straits: 39, 41, 42.
    legal nature of: 42, 43.
    and territorial sovereignty: 43, 44.
    freedom of navigation in: 44–45.
    permanency of regime in: 45.
    and other regimes: 46, 47.
International Commission of Paris. See Conference of Paris of 1885.
International Commission of the Oder Case: 23, 40, 46.
International Conventions and third States: 30. See Stipulations in favour of third States.
International Court of Justice:
    and international straits: 34, 41.
    and international settlements: 33, 34.

and tacit consent: 35.
acceptance by Egypt of compulsory
jurisdiction of: 20, 108.
proposal for compulsory jurisdiction
of: 113.
International Law Commission: 38.
International public utility, doctrine of:
37, 38.
International Rivers:
definition: 22, 23.
relation to international straits and
canals: 39, 41, 42.
legal nature of: 39, 40.
and warships: 45.
International Settlements:
concept of: 33.
existence of: 33, 34, 39.
and the Constantinople Convention of
1888: 76–80, 86, 87.
International Status of South-West
Africa Case: 33.
International Straits: 22.
definition of: 23, 24.
relation to international rivers and
canals: 39, 41, 42.
legal nature of: 40, 41.
International Waterways: 1, 22, 26.
Interoceanic Canals:
and legal theory: 1.
traffic in: 2.
Inter-Parliamentary Union: 1.
Invasion of 1956, Anglo-French: 3, 20,
108.
Invasion of 1956, Israeli: 3, 19.
Ismail Pasha, Khedive of Egypt: 8.
Israeli-Egyptian War of 1956: 3, 19, 20.
Isthmus of Suez: 4, 5, 10, 63.
Italo-Abyssinian War of 1935–36: 15,
87.
Italo-Turkish War of 1911–12: 79.

Kiel Canal: 1, 26, 27.
and Treaty of Versailles: 33, 36.
and German Proclamation: 36, 37.
and freedom of navigation: 44.
Kiel Canal Collision Case: 26, 37, 42, 43.

Le Père, J. M.: 4.
Lesseps, Ferdinand de:
and the granting of the Concessions: 5.
and Sultan's ratification: 6.
and organization of the Suez Canal
Co.: 7, 49, 50, 52.
and agreement with Colonel Stokes:
56.
attemps to internationalize the Suez
Canal: 61.
proposals for neutralizing the Suez
Canal: 62, 63.

and British landing on the Isthmus
of Suez: 10, 63.
and legal status of the Suez Canal Co.:
91, 92, 98, 102.
and sovereignty over the Canal: 94.
and sale of the Canal: 95.

Mac Donald, Prime Minister: 15.
Marquis Becquehem Case: 81, 82.
Marshall, General: 84.
Maxwell, Sir John: 13.
Mehemet Ali, Viceroy of Egypt: 4, 5.
Military Proclamation of Sept. 4, 1939:
83.
Milner, Lord: 14.
Minimum Standard Rule: 102.
Minquiers and Ecrehos Case: 35.
Mixed Court of Appeal of Egypt: 44.
Mixed Court of Appeals of Alexandria:
92.
Multilateral treaties:
and establishment of international
canals: 29, 30.
and non-acceding States: 30–35.

Napoleon I: 4.
Napoleon III: 6, 7, 50.
Nasser, President:
and Egyptian sovereignty: 3.
and nationalization of the Suez Canal
Co.: 18, 89, 90, 93, 102, 103, 106.
and Five-Power Proposal: 19, 101,
107.
National canal, definition of: 26.
Nationalization of the Suez Canal Co.: 3.
meaning of: 18.
right of: 102, 106.
international repercussions of: 3, 18,
19, 90.
and international rights: 99, 102, 106,
107.
Newcastle Chamber of Commerce: 61.
Note of January 4, 1860: 6, 52.
Note of April 6, 1863: 6, 52.
Note of December 20, 1945: 16, 17.
Note of May 28, 1947: 84, 86, 87.
Note sur la juridiction dans l'Isthme: 94.
Notification of Oct. 23, 1914: 81.

Opinio necessitatis iuris: 87.

Pacta tertiis nec prosunt nec nocent: 30.
Palestinian War of 1948: 17, 85, 86, 87,
88, 105.
Panama Canal: 1, 2, 34.
Paris Commission of 1885. See Confer
ence of Paris of 1885.
Pauncefote, Sir Julian: 11.
Permanent Court of International Jus-
tice:

and international rivers: 23, 40.
and international canals: 25, 26, 43, 44, 45.
and Kiel Canal: 36, 44.
and Suez Canal: 71, 72.
and unilateral declarations: 27.
and stipulations favourable to a third party: 30–31.
and international settlements: 33.
and abuse of rights: 38.
and regime of internationalization: 46.
Pharaohs, The: 4.
Pindos Case: 82.
Practice of States and the Constantinople Convention of 1888:
before World War I: 78, 79, 80.
from World War I to World War II: 80, 81, 82, 83.
from World War II to date: 83–87.
Presidential Decree of July 26, 1956. See Nationalization of the Suez Canal Co.
Privy Council: 82.
Prize Council of Egypt: 85.
Proclamation of August 5, 1914: 80.
Proclamation of May 15, 1948: 85.
Proclamation of Nov. 14, 1936: 36, 37.
Protectorate over Egypt, British: 13, 82, 83.
Protocol of London of 1841: 5.

Question of tonnage measurement: 55, 56.

Regime of demilitarization:
definition of: 46.
and the Suez Canal before 1888: 62.
and the Constantinople Convention of 1888: 69, 70.
and the practice of States: 83, 84, 87.
Regime of internationality:
definition of: 46, 57.
origin of: 60, 97, 98, 101.
results of: 73, 96, 97, 98, 104.
and international canals: 48.
and Suez Canal: 49, 57, 58.
and the Great Powers: 59.
and other regimes before 1888: 62, 64, 65.
and the Convention of Constantinople of 1888: 66, 70, 73, 89.
Regime of internationalization:
definition of: 46, 61.
and the Suez Canal before 1888: 61, 62,100.
and the Constantinople Convention of 1888: 69, 70, 71, 82, 87, 112.
and the Tripartite Statement: 107.
Regime of neutralization:
definition of: 46, 47.

and the Suez Canal before 1888: 61, 62, 63, 64.
and the Constantinople Convention of 1888: 68–73, 76, 80, 89, 112.
Règlement pour la Libre Navigation des Rivières: 22.
Reparation for Injuries Suffered in the Service of the U.N. Case: 34, 35.
Res inter alios acta: 86.
Revolution of 1952 in Egypt: 17, 18.
Roosevelt, President: 84.
Rules regarding Coaling by Belligerent Warships in the Suez Canal of Feb. 10, 1904: 79.
Russo-Japanese War of 1904: 71, 79.
Russo-Turkish War of 1877: 9, 58, 63.

Said Pasha, Viceroy of Egypt: 5, 6.
Salisbury, Lord: 70.
Seymour, Admiral: 9.
Sinai Incident: 13.
Sinai Peninsula: 13, 20.
Spanish-American War of 1898: 70, 71, 78.
Stipulatio in favorem tertii: 32.
Stipulations in favour of third States:
recognized by the P.C.I.J.: 30–31.
followed by acceptance: 31–32.
not followed by acceptance: 32.
and international settlements: 33–34.
and custom: 34, 35.
and the Constantinople Convention of 1888: 75, 76, 87.
Stokes, Colonel: 56.
Suez Canal:
opening of: 1, 7.
reasons for its success: 1, 2, 3, 4.
traffic through: 2, 8, 10.
ancient history of: 4, 5.
construction and recent history of: 6, 8.
and Russo-Turkish War: 9.
demand for a second canal: 10.
British occupation and security of: 12, 15.
Sinai incident and security of: 13.
British Claim to protect the Canal: 15.
and World War I: 80, 81.
and World War II: 16, 83, 84.
and Palestinian War of 1948: 85.
and Anglo-French invasion: 20.
reopened to navigation: 20.
legal status of, before 1888: 48–57, 64.
Viceroy's consent needed: 49–51.
Sultan's consent needed: 51, 52, 53, 54.
Sultan's consent to establishment of international regime in: 54, 55, 56, 57.
status of, according to the Concessions: 57, 58.

regime of internationality before 1888: 59, 60.
status of, according to Egyptian Government: 59, 60.
and various usages: 58, 59, 61.
attempts to internationalize: 61.
proposals for sale of: 61, 95.
regime of demilitarization before 1888: 62.
regime of neutralization before 1888: 62, 63.
Egyptian sovereignty over: 93, 94, 95, 103, 104.
Egyptian property of: 95, 96.
administration of: 96, 104, 105, 106.
right of passage through: 96, 97, 98, 104, 106.
regime of internationalization in: 107.
Egyptian guarantees with regard to: 108, 109, 110.
Suez Canal Base: 15, 18, 103.
Suez Canal Board: 107.
Suez Canal Commission of 1885. See Conference of Paris of 1885.
Suez Canal Company:
establishment of: 2, 5, 6, 91.
universal character of: 3, 91.
privileges of: 5–6.
organization of: 7–8.
financial difficulties of: 61.
purchase of shares by Great Britain: 8, 99.
legal status of: 7, 102.
Egyptian character of: 91, 92, 93.
and regime of internationality: 97, 98.
and Art. 14 of the 1856 Concession: 51.
and the Constantinople Convention of 1888: 100, 101, 102, 103.
nationalization of: 3, 18, 89, 90, 102, 106, 107.
compensation to shareholders of: 20.
and the Tripartite Statement: 90, 91, 93, 99.
as agency of the international community: 93, 99, 100, 102.
and sovereignty over the Canal: 94.
and property of the Canal: 95, 96.
and administration of the Canal: 96, 104, 105, 106.
Suez Canal Users Association: 19, 107.
Suez Canal Zone Base. See Suez Canal Base.
Suez Question:
elements of: 93–98, 101, 103, 104, 105.
Egyptian declaration regarding: 108, 109, 110.
ways of solving the: 111, 112, 113.
System of tolerance: 60, 61.

Tacit Acceptance and the Constantinople Convention of 1888: 76, 87.
Tacit Consent: 35, 36, 39.
Tel-el-Kebir, Battle at: 10.
Tewfik, Viceroy of Egypt: 9.
Tolls in the Suez Canal: 55, 58, 59, 112.
Tonnage measurement in the Suez Canal: 55, 56, 58.
Trail Smelter Arbitration Case: 38.
Treaties of Peace of 1919 and British Protectorate over Egypt: 13, 82.
Treaty of: August 26, 1936
conclusion of: 15, 16.
discussion of, in the Sec. Council: 17.
termination of: 18.
effects of: 83, 94, 103.
Constantinople of 1888. See Convention of.
Hay-Pauncefote: 34.
Lausanne of 1923: 13, 82, 103.
October 19, 1954: 15, 18, 74, 103.
peace and establishment of internat. regime in canals: 36, 37.
St. Germain: 13, 75, 82.
Trianon: 13, 75, 82.
Versailles:
and international rivers: 23.
and Kiel Canal: 25, 26, 33, 36, 44.
and Hitler: 36–37.
and British Protectorate over Egypt: 82.
Tribunal de Cassation of France: 92.
Tribunal de Commerce de la Seine: 92.
Tripartite Statement of August 2, 1956: 90, 91, 93, 99, 102, 103, 107.
Turkish Circular Letter of Jan. 1, 1873: 55.
Turkish Circular Letter of May 1918: 81.
Turkish Note of Jan. 4, 1860: 6, 52.
Turkish Note of April 6, 1863: 6, 52.

Ultimatum, Anglo-French: 20.
Unilateral Declarations:
recognized by the P. C. I. J.: 27.
and opinion of writers: 27–28.
modes of: 29.
acceptance of: 29.
and establishment of international canals: 28–29, 39, 42, 43.
and Suez Canal: 48, 49.
United Nations and internationalization of canals: 46.
U. N. Emergency Force: 20.
U. N. General Assembly: 20.
U. N. Secretariat: 108, 109.
U. N. Security Council:
discusses 1936 Treaty: 17.
and nationalization of Suez Canal Co.: 19.

and Anglo-French invasion: 20.
and Constantinople Convention of 1888: 65, 75, 85, 87, 104.
and international status of Suez Canal: 59, 60, 74, 99, 100.
and Suez Question: 95, 99, 108, 109, 110.
Resolution of Oct. 13, 1956 of: 108, 123.
Universal Company of the Maritime Canal of Suez. See Suez Canal Co.
U. S. Department of State: 18, 79.

Wafd party: 14.
War of 1870 between France and Germany: 58, 63.
1877 between Turkey and Russia: 9, 58, 63.
1898 between Spain and the U.S.A.: 70, 71, 78.
1904 between Japan and Russia: 71, 79.
1911 between Italy and Turkey: 79.
1914 (World War I): 13, 80, 81, 82, 84, 87, 88.
1935 between Italy and Ethiopia: 15, 87.
1939 (World War II): 16, 83, 84, 87, 88.
1948 between Israel and the Arab States: 17, 85, 86, 87, 88, 105.
1956 between Israel and Egypt: 3, 19, 20.
Wimbledon Case: 25, 26, 33, 36, 43, 44, 45, 71, 72.
World Bank: 18.
Wosley, General: 10.

Zaghlul Pasha: 14, **15**

DATE DUE